The kicks just keep getting harder to find . . .

- A repentant thief sends 14 women in Salt Lake City their stolen lingerie.

- An Ohio woman awakens to fleeing burglars—and her rear end covered with whipped cream and sugar.

- An outraged Kentucky man shoots his uncle for romancing a pit bull.

- Chinese prostitutes aged 70 to 93 are jailed for breaking the terms of their pensions by continuing to service 200 clients a month.

- A Connecticut man offers women free samples of panties in exchange for leaving their used underwear in mailbox for pickup.

- Two voyeuristic airline passengers throw food at a stewardess in an attempt to stop her from interrupting two other passengers engaged in oral sex.

From the St. Louis "Birdman" who fondles women then runs off flapping his arms, to the Florida cop found frisking the breasts of dozens of female drivers, here are 100 percent true-news accounts guaranteed to outrage the moral minority and just plain tickle the rest of us!

JOHN J. KOHUT is a political analyst and writer in Washington, D.C. He has been collecting strange news clippings for more than two decades. ROLAND SWEET is a magazine editor and the author of his own syndicated column. Kohut and Sweet are co-authors of the News of the Weird series, the Dumb, Dumber, Dumbest series, and *Strange Tails*, available in Plume.

REAL SEX

Titillating but True Tales of Bizarre Fetishes, Strange Compulsions, and Just Plain Weird Stuff

John J. Kohut
and
Roland Sweet

A PLUME BOOK

PLUME
Published by the Penguin Group
Penguin Putnam Inc., 375 Hudson Street, New York, New York 10014, U.S.A.
Penguin Books Ltd, 27 Wrights Lane, London W8 5TZ, England
Penguin Books Australia Ltd, Ringwood, Victoria, Australia
Penguin Books Canada Ltd, 10 Alcorn Avenue, Toronto, Ontario, Canada M4V 3B2
Penguin Books (N.Z.) Ltd, 182–190 Wairau Road, Auckland 10, New Zealand

Penguin Books Ltd, Registered Offices:
Harmondsworth, Middlesex, England

First published by Plume, an imprint of Penguin Putnam Inc.

First Printing, January, 2000
10 9 8 7 6 5 4 3 2 1

 REGISTERED TRADEMARK—MARCA REGISTRADA

LIBRARY OF CONGRESS CATALOGING-IN-PUBLICATION DATA:

Real sex : titillating but true tales of bizarre fetishes, strange
  compulsions, and just plain weird stuff / compiled by John J. Kohut
  & Roland Sweet.
      p.   cm.
    ISBN 0-452-28151-2
    1. Sex—Miscellanea.   2. Sex—Anecdotes.   I. Kohut, John J.
  II. Sweet, Roland.
  HQ25.R43   2000
  306.7—dc21   99-36229
                                                         CIP

Printed in the United States of America
Set in Century Book
Designed by Leonard Telesca

Contents

Introduction

If you think the things that Bill and Monica did are kinky, all we can say is close but no cigar. They're a couple of straitlaced Puritans compared to some of the goings-on and comings we uncovered compiling this chronicle of sexual folly. They lead us to one inescapable conclusion: Men aren't called *Homo erectus* because they walk upright.

Indeed, men and women, no matter how civilized they think they are, are slaves to their hormones. The urge to merge is more compelling than most of us would dare admit.

After reading these 600 true stories, you'll no longer wonder why the president and Miss Lewinsky did what they did. You'll actually admire their restraint.

We stress that all the items in this hefty volume are authentic. They appeared in legitimate news sources. We have not embellished them or spiced up any of the language. We have avoided incidents that were so well covered everyone can recite the details. For example, we do not recount the Lorena and John Wayne Bobbitt saga. Why bother? Our chapter "Little Things Mean a Lot" contains dozens of penis amputations, some of them self-inflicted.

Some of our accounts are humorous, others are gruesome. A few are downright shocking. Even to us. And,

after digging through 15 years' worth of newspapers looking for these oddities, we don't blush easily.

Beyond shock value or mere titillation, we believe that
these news reports, taken as a whole, offer evidence of
what it means to be human. Horny!

—John J. Kohut
Roland Sweet

Dumb Sex

Darryl Washington and Maria Ramos were injured at New York City's Bowery subway station when a train plowed into them while they were having sex on a mattress they had thrown on the tracks.

Three months after his indictment on charges stemming from having sex with a 15-year-old girl, Edward J. Jeffords, 21, of Perryville, Maryland, appeared with three of his friends on *The Jerry Springer Show* to tout the advantages of having sex with minors. "You must have rocks in your head," Cecil County Circuit Judge Dexter M. Thompson Jr. told Jeffords just before sentencing him to five years in prison. "Not only do you do this, do the offense, get indicted, and then you go on the show and talk about it."

A jury in Nashville, Tennessee, convicted Raymond Mitchell III, 45, of tricking women into blindfolding themselves and having sex with him by claiming to be their boyfriend. Prosecutors said most of the hundreds of women that Mitchell called hung up, but of the 30 women who reported the encounters to police, eight said they had sex with the caller. One woman admitted having sex with the man twice a week over two months until she discovered he wasn't her boyfriend during one encounter when her blindfold slipped off.

Rosaline A. Kelly sued the former Spring Street Tavern in Chippewa Falls, Wisconsin, after she had consensual exhibitionistic sex with two men, claiming that the bartender and manager failed to prevent her from acting irresponsibly. The court ruled against her.

A man checked into the hospital complaining of pain in his scrotum. A West Chester, Pennsylvania, urologist reported in the journal *Medical Aspects of Human Sexuality* that the scrotum was swollen and lacerated. The patient explained that he worked in a machine shop and during his lunch hour masturbated by holding his penis against a canvas drive belt. As he neared climax, he leaned too close and the machine tore his scrotum. He compounded the problem by trying to close the wound with a heavy-duty stapler.

Despite having the world's largest population, mandatory family planning (one child per couple), and one of the longest traditions of erotic literature, China has many well-educated people who don't know how babies are made, according to Jiang Yunfen, vice president of the Shanghai Sex Education Research Society. "We've had childless college professors who come in after being married for several years," she said, "and they still believe that if they just lie down together and fall asleep, they will produce a baby." The society acted to correct the problem by sponsoring the city's first public sex-education exhibit, which featured tiny clay figures demonstrating four lovemaking positions.

Doctors in Singapore who were curious about the country's infertility problem discovered that many couples don't know how to have sex. According to Dr. Ganesan Adaikan of the Society for the Study of Andrology and Sexology, "When a couple does not know how to engage in sexual intercourse, it results in infertility."

Romanian first division soccer player Mario Bugeanu, 24, and his 23-year-old girlfriend Mirela Iancu died after having sex in his car in a garage with the motor running. "They appeared to be unaware of the dangers of carbon monoxide," police colonel Dumitru Secrieru said.

Police in Stevens Point, Wisconsin, arrested Della Dobbs, 31, for theft, accusing her of meeting men in bars, then taking them outside to her pickup truck to have sex. Before beginning, she persuaded the men to take off their clothes, get out, and rub themselves with snow to get sexually aroused. While they complied, she would drive off with their wallets.

Lars Bildman, the chief executive of the pharmaceutical company Astra USA, was fired following accusations that he replaced older women with younger, more attractive women, pressured female employees to have sex, and embezzled $2 million. But Astra board member Lars Ramqvist was quoted in the Swedish magazine

Maanadens Affaerer as saying: "Of course it's not good with sex scandals, but in the U.S. this has helped us get out Astra's name without having to pay expensive advertising fees."

The lawyer for a 24-year-old man accused of raping his 40-year-old mother-in-law in Glen Burnie, Maryland, got his client acquitted by claiming "sex by mistake." The mother-in-law said she thought he was her husband and didn't realize he wasn't until some 30 minutes after they had sex. The son-in-law claimed he mistook her for his wife, even though he and his wife lived several miles away.

Mohammed Abdel Rahman, 29, leaped to his death from a Cairo balcony on his wedding night when he learned that his mother-in-law had switched brides, tricking him into marrying the uglier of her two daughters. Rahman had had to leave the country on business and entrusted the wedding paperwork to his brother and the mother-in-law, who wrote the other daughter's name on the forms.

Police arrested John Dawson, 26, in South St. Paul, Minnesota, for breaking into a young woman's apartment in an elaborate scheme to have sex with her. The authorities said that just before she arrived, he left a note on her kitchen table instructing her to go into her bedroom immediately and have sex with him because a man with a gun had kidnapped him and was waiting to kill another person if she refused. Then he undressed, put duct tape over his eyes, handcuffed himself to her bed, and waited.

When the woman arrived home and read the note, she went straight to the police. Dawson tried to free himself, but he had left the key to the handcuffs on the kitchen table before he handcuffed himself to the bed, where police found him when they arrived.

Sex Is Its Own Punishment

After picking up money from a bank in Dayton, Ohio, Wells Fargo armored car driver Aaron McKie decided to engage the services of a prostitute. They had sex in the vehicle, FBI Agent Peter A. Lakes noted, adding that after the "female exited the armored van, McKie noticed that the bag with the bank's $80,000 was missing." When McKie reported the incident, he lost his job.

Doctors at Baltimore's Johns Hopkins Hospital reported treating two men, ages 75 and 72, who lost their memory after having sex. Writing in the journal *The Lancet*, hematologists Chi Van Dang and Lawrence B. Gardner said the men's wives took them to the hospital when they became seriously confused. The doctors concluded that the memory loss resulted from the men overexerting themselves, which created intense pressure in blood vessels in their brains that temporarily blocked blood flow, causing amnesia that lasted six to twelve hours. Dang and Gardner suggested that other men may experience similar temporary memory loss.

Twenty-year-old Daisy Gladden was hospitalized in Akron, Ohio, for hypothermia after spending four days underneath a man who died just after they had sex in the front seat of a car. After her rescue, the woman explained, "I just thought he was a hard sleeper."

While dropping her husband off for work in Maine, Sherry Moeller gave him a kiss next to the car and flashed her breasts. The Hong Kong *Standard* reported that cab driver Tim Vegas saw her and lost control of his vehicle, running over the curb and into the Johnson Medical Building, knocking loose a piece of mortar that fell on Moeller. Inside the building, dental technician Pamela Klesick was cleaning Bryan Corcoran's teeth when the crash startled her, causing her to tear Corcoran's gums with a cleaning pick; he in turn bit down, severing two fingers from Klesick's hand. "I'm not sure why I did it," Moeller said afterward. "I was really close to the car, so I didn't think anyone would see it."

Michael Guilbault, 19, and an accomplice were arrested for robbing a convenience store in Raleigh, North Carolina, after they raced to their getaway car but found the other two members of their gang, Curtis Johnson, 19, and Heather Beckwith, 18, inside with the doors locked having sex. According to the prosecutor, Guilbault, who pleaded guilty, and his accomplice were forced to wait until the couple finished before they could get in the car, by which time their pacing and yelling had attracted the attention of several witnesses.

Oscar Dominguez, 45, a São Paulo psychiatrist, admitted shooting a woman patient to death after she attempted to tell him about her sex life. He told the court, "I couldn't take those nut cases anymore."

A woman in Long Branch, New Jersey, was hospitalized briefly after she performed a striptease for her boyfriend with a shotgun and accidentally shot herself in one of her breasts.

Officials at Great Park near England's Windsor Castle reported that a woman was treated for a broken leg after she fell naked from an oak tree while having sex. "As they reached the height of their passion, the woman slipped from one of the branches at the top of the tree and plunged to the ground," a park spokesperson explained. "It was a very clear case of coitus interruptus."

A couple had to be treated for hypothermia in Gernsheim, Germany, after the parked car in which they were having sex rolled down a boat ramp into the Rhine River.

Two Indonesian villagers accused of committing adultery were marched to the village chief's house, where a security official beat them, made them undress, and forced them to have sex twice in public.

An Italian couple filed a suit against an insurance company, blaming the woman's pregnancy on an automobile accident. According to a Naples newspaper, the couple claimed they were making out in a car in a popular lover's lane when another car rammed theirs from behind, causing the couple to "lose control and be unable to avoid insemination."

The federal government reported that some 250,000 of the 10.7 million U.S. women who take oral contraceptives become pregnant because they fail to follow directions properly.

During an extended drought in the North African nation of Niger, police arrested 16 people after catching them having sex in dried-up cattle troughs. Police acted against the couples when Muslim clerics in Nkonni village complained that "illicit" activities were hampering the effectiveness of collective prayers for rain.

Passengers aboard a train from Margate, England, to London ignored a couple that engaged in oral sex in a first-class compartment, then moved to a packed second-class compartment and performed "full sexual intercourse." But when they had finished and lit cigarettes, several passengers became annoyed and complained to the conductor because the compartment was designated nonsmoking. The conductor radioed ahead to police, who met the train and arrested John Henderson, 29, and Zoe D'Arcy, 19. The couple were each fined $142 for violating the smoking regulation and committing an indecent act.

Cherry Florence, a high school teacher in Milford, Utah, was fired for sharing a list with her students that purportedly identified which boys and girls in grades 9 through 12 had been sexually active and which ones hadn't.

A 38-year-old man reported that he was robbed by another man he met in a Salt Lake City bar, telling police the suspect asked him for a ride home, during which the two discussed sexual matters and then began fondling each other. The victim stopped the car, and the two were groping each other when the suspect grabbed the victim's $300 Gucci watch from his wrist and fled. The victim, who was intoxicated at the time, said he didn't get a good look at the suspect's face but insisted he could identify him by the smell of his cologne and by holding his genitals.

The widow of a USAir pilot, who claimed her husband's fatal brain hemorrhage was really an accident caused by having sex with another woman, lost her suit against his insurance company seeking accidental death benefits. U.S. District Judge John Kane ruled that sex is "not an accident as contemplated in the law."

Seven people in Washington, D.C., were seriously injured in a three-car pileup, including a dazed and drunken man and woman that police found naked from the waist down. "They were involved in some sort of sexual activity," Deputy Chief Melvin Clark explained. "Evidently, things got out of control."

The sex act involved the couple in the front seat and

another man in the back seat while the compact car was idling. Officials said that the man in the front seat apparently had his foot on the gas pedal, and at some point someone knocked the gearshift out of park and the car sped through a stop sign onto a main street, where the collision occurred.

Police in Israel charged a motorist with reckless driving after witnessing him driving down a coastal highway while having sex with a woman. Both were naked when they were pulled over. The driver explained that he had picked up the woman hitchhiking and that "she was a pretty girl and I forgot myself."

A 76-year-old Georgia woman who claimed her 72-year-old husband's throat was slashed by an intruder later admitted that the killer was a hitchhiker whom they had brought home to have sex with the wife while the husband watched. "They picked the guy up for sex, but the guy decided he didn't want sex," Clayton County Police Captain Danny Westbrooks said. "He wanted their car and some money."

Of the estimated 114 million acts of sexual intercourse that occur daily, 356,000 result in the transmission of viral or bacterial infections, according to the International Planned Parenthood Federation. Some 910,000 of the sex acts result in conception, of which only 390,000 are carried to term.

One Pill Makes You Larger

A report issued by the federal Food and Drug Administration listed the following possible side effects of the anti-impotence drug Viagra: "Abnormal hair growth, speech disorder, amnesia, loss of libido, hallucination, anorexia, tinnitus, skin discoloration, hiccups, sleepwalking, eye-rolling hostility, euphoric mood, dry mouth, agitation, confusion, insomnia, abnormal thinking, abnormal skin odor, depression, increased sweating, flatulence, abnormal dreams, and belching."

Viagra was credited with increasing business at several Nevada brothels. Joe Richards, owner of the Cherry Patch and Mabel's, reported that his business rose some 10 percent after the pill went on the market. "We have a lot of guys who used to come up here but stopped, and now they're back," he said. "The girls say they're on the pill."

Larry Demorest, 89, was charged with attempted murder in Orlando, Florida, after the victim told sheriff's deputies that Demorest popped a Viagra, then tried to kill her when she refused to perform sex for money. Demorest admitted his doctor prescribed the anti-impotence pill but denied the charge, explaining that a recent case of shingles has reined in his libido. "I might look good, but I'm still pushing a hundred," he said.

Roberta Burke, 63, filed a $2-million palimony suit in New York Supreme Court in Mineola against her common-law husband, Francis Bernardo, 70, claiming that he left her for another woman after Viagra cured his impotence. Burke's suit said that an hour after Bernardo took the little blue pill, they had sex for the first time in four years. Two days later, he left, telling her, "It's time for me to be a stud again."

After reading that some insurance companies and state health programs refused to cover Viagra, Alan "Ace" Greenberg, head of the investment firm Bear, Stearns and Company, announced that he was giving $1 million to New York City's Hospital for Special Surgery to buy the pill, which sells for $8 to $10, for men who cannot afford it. "I made the money," Greenberg said, "and I'm going to give it away any way I want to."

Elcio Berti, the mayor of Bocaiuva do Sul, Brazil, announced that he had spent $35,000 of his own money to buy enough Viagra to hand out 4,000 free samples to "those in need" in an effort to boost the town's population. He explained that unless the town's population rose from 10,000 to 12,000 federal aid would fall from $110,000 to $70,000 a year. "Expenses are going up, and revenue is falling," said Berti, whose attempt the previous year to outlaw condoms was ruled unconstitutional. "There is nothing else I can do."

The first lawsuit against the maker of Viagra was filed by Diego Padro, 63, who claimed he had a heart attack after several days of sex using the drug. "Viagra changed my life but not favorably," Padro said after filing his $85-million suit in New York Supreme Court against Pfizer, Inc. "No one needs to improve their sex life to the point where they might die."

Joseph Moran, a used car salesman from Middlesex County, New Jersey, filed another lawsuit against Pfizer, seeking $10 million. He claimed that after he took Viagra for recreational use, he saw blue streaks shooting from his fingers, insisting the side effect caused him to crash his car.

The Federal Aviation Administration recommended that pilots not take Viagra within six hours of flying because the drug might interfere with their ability to distinguish between the colors blue and green. Blue lights are used to outline airport taxiways, and green lights illuminate aircraft digital instrument panels. Writing in the *Federal Air Surgeon's Medical Bulletin*, flight surgeon Dr. Donato J. Borrillo warned that "full attention to the instrument scan and the task at hand may be compromised" by Viagra.

When Viagra was introduced in Thailand, Pfizer officials made a point of announcing that the drug would not prolong sex. According to a recent survey, Thais spend the least time having sex: 10.4 minutes per encounter.

Viagra could cost France's state health system up to $55 million a year, according to Solidarity and Employment Minister Martine Aubry. Although the state will not reimburse users for the drug, doctors' visits are covered. The government estimated that at the time of its approval, an additional 500,000 Frenchmen sought prescriptions for the drug.

Fearing Viagra would cost the Defense Department $50 million that it had not anticipated, it asked Congress to bolster its budget to provide the drug for active-duty and retired service personnel. After military officials told Congress it didn't include the amount in that year's budget request, Pentagon spokesperson Jim Turner explained, "Viagra sort of burst on the scene."

After withdrawing his savings, pawning his wedding ring, and taking out a loan, Romanian Georgio Barrsan, 56, spent the money on black-market Viagra and two prostitutes. He took six of the pills but then fell asleep. He awoke 12 hours later to find the women and his wallet gone. Investigators discovered that instead of Viagra, Barrsan had been sold sleeping pills.

A United Arab Emirates national with 46 children advised his countrymen to forget about Viagra and eat plenty of fish instead. According to the Emirates News, Ahmed Rashid bin Aboud, 48, who lives in the emirate of Fujairah on the UAE's east coast, said he had 23 sons and 23 daughters from eight wives, one of whom had given birth to 17 children. "Eat fish, and more fish," Aboud told the paper. "I spend fifty-four dollars every day on fish."

Classic Pickup Lines

Barry Alan Briskman, 57, seduced two 13-year-old girls in Los Angeles by claiming that he was from the planet Cablell and promising them a ride in his spaceship. He told them that he had been sent to Earth to recruit a "team" of beautiful girls of high intelligence to travel to Cablell and join the female-dominated society there. In order to be ready for the trip, he said, each girl had to double her IQ and break down her "sub-cons," or subconscious. After games of strip poker to break down "sub-cons," the man then convinced each girl to begin having sex with him so that he could inject them with "IRFs"—immunities that would deter space diseases. After each sex session, the man dialed the Cablellian computer Andrak 4000, which would issue a readout on each girl's "sub-con" and "IRF" levels. A total of 100 "IRFs" was needed for space travel.

"He's a classic pedophile," said one police detective after the man was sentenced to 20 years in state prison.

A Cincinnati woman reported that she was sexually assaulted by a man who took advantage of her tendency to faint whenever she hears the word *sex*. The woman told police that the 42-year-old man learned of her condition, spoke the word to her, and molested her twice while she was unconscious. According to the accused man's attorney, Paul Tellez, the woman passed out twice during a court hearing when the word *sex* was mentioned.

Police in Simsbury, Connecticut, arrested a 44-year-old man after he tried to trick a woman into giving him her used underwear. The man telephoned the woman and explained that he represented a company giving away free samples of underwear to women who would turn in their used underwear in exchange. All she had to do was leave her underwear in a bag in her mailbox. Police had the woman leave towels instead and arrested him when he removed the bag from the mailbox. Inside his car, police discovered a list of 240 women, with each woman's address, height, age, and underwear size meticulously recorded.

Thirteen women in Midwest City, Oklahoma, complained that a 28-year-old man looked up their dresses while he was interviewing them for a job. The man conned the local library into giving him a library room in which to conduct interviews for a fictitious secretarial job with a fictitious Jaycees organization. At a certain point during the interview he required each woman to undergo the "Johnson Stress Test." At that point he blindfolded each woman and made them take dictation from a tape recording. They had to assume three positions—sitting on a desk, standing with feet apart and pad in hand, and bending over the pad on the desk. It was during this test that he apparently looked up their dresses. Upon investigation, police determined that he had pulled the same stunt in other nearby city libraries, conducting "interviews" for three-hour and eight-hour sessions.

Over a four-year period in the late 1980s, a mystery telephone caller known as the "spanking phantom" contacted baby-sitters and day care providers in and around Eau Claire, Wisconsin, inquiring if they would be willing to spank immature children and adults. Claiming to work for a federally funded program, the man said that his "subjects," between the ages of seven and 40, were immature and "in need of discipline" requiring spanking on their "bare bottoms." He then would ask the baby-sitters to describe in great detail just how they would discipline and spank his subjects. Police attempts to trace the phone calls failed.

Karen L. Wrobel, 43, of La Crosse, Wisconsin, was charged with illegal sexual contact with a 15-year-old boy. The prosecutor in the case said the woman seduced the boy by telling him she had a bubble in her brain that could pop and kill her if the boy turned her down.

A San Luis Obispo, California, man phoned an apartment where four young women lived and asked if they'd go along with a stunt he had to perform as a fraternity pledge. He explained that he had to strip in front of them and parade before them in women's underwear. Her suspicions raised, one of the women called the local chapter of Theta Chi and asked if any such pledge stunt was going on. The fraternity said that they had heard several reports of someone using their name in similar scenarios and agreed to set a trap. On the appointed night, the man arrived at the apartment, entered the bathroom, and emerged in a see-through negligee. Dancing for the room-

mates, he handed them a note saying that they were supposed to spank him, and he indicated the wooden paddle
he had brought along. A Theta Chi member hiding in a
bedroom phoned the police.

A Texas school superintendent resigned after a Dallas
television station videotaped him entering and leaving
several adult bookstores and movie theaters, spending
several hours at a visit. He insisted that he was actually
running his own investigation as to whether other school
employees were inside such businesses.

A Hong Kong court convicted former police officer
Sham Kwok-keung of "unlawful sex acts by false pretens-
es" after he posed as a doctor and convinced a 41-year-old
woman that having sex with him was the only way to prevent other doctors from cutting off her husband's penis.

After the Reverend Joseph Millien was arrested in
Delray Beach, Florida, for molesting a young girl, he
insisted that he was only checking to make sure she was
a virgin. Millien admitted he had no medical expertise
about how to determine that she was.

Prosecutors at the sexual abuse trial of Navajo medicine
man Yazzie King, 63, in Albuquerque, New Mexico,
charged that King convinced women they had objects and
evil spirits inside them and to let him use a bamboo flute
to suck the evil spirits out of their genitals.

Four women bystanders standing in a crowd of people watching the aftermath of an auto accident in Takoma Park, Maryland, were approached by a man in a jogging suit who claimed to be a doctor, and asked to check their pulses and feel their chests. The four cooperated but contacted police later that night.

A 14-year-old boy in Wolverhampton, England, dressed in his school uniform, rode his bike to the home of a 48-year-old woman. Posing as a doctor, he convinced her to have sex with him on the pretense that it would confirm the results of a cervical cancer smear test. Prosecutors said that the boy overheard that the woman had had a smear test at a local clinic and called her on the phone to say that he was sending an assistant to her home to have sex with her. The woman testified that she "did not realize what I was doing."

An Oklahoma State University student was put on a year's probation for an incident in which, posing as a campus maintenance man, he entered a woman's apartment and pushed her into a bathtub filled with water. The 23-year-old engineering student claimed that he was conducting a survey to determine how many women he could trick into letting him into their home.

A woman in Bay City, Texas, allowed a doctor to spank her over a period of two months (in at least 16 spanking sessions, some lasting as long as 90 minutes) before going to police to complain that he had not paid her the promised $2,500 fee that he said she would earn for participating in his "pain research project." The Texas Board of Medical Examiners then filed a complaint against the doctor after they determined that the research project did not exist and that the physician had developed the story just to convince women to come in for spanking sessions.

Further investigation found that the Louisiana state medical board had earlier suspended the doctor's license to practice in that state under similar circumstances. In the Texas case, the doctor told women that the research was being funded by the manufacturer of a major pain-relief medication and that the research required him to find their "pain threshold." The doctor spanked the women with his hand, a belt, an extension cord, and a wooden board.

A London minister and police chaplain, described as a "gifted preacher," was convicted of luring young girls into posing naked for him by telling them they would be illustrating "kidnap and rescue" stories for the church magazine.

A former Fordham University student filed a lawsuit claiming that Julio M. Soto, a doctor associated with the school, had told her two years before that she had herpes and could be cured by a secret vaccine. He convinced her that the vaccine would work best if she had sex just before it was administered with the person administering it.

Police in Oakland, California, reported they were seeking a man who preyed on women immigrants by phoning them, saying he was from a clinic, and telling them they carried a rare germ. To avoid being deported, they would have to undergo special treatment. He would be injected with a serum (for which the immigrant had to pay $650), which could then be passed to the victim only through sexual intercourse.

A Queens, New York, woman sued her former psychiatrist for $5 million, charging that he seduced her into a sexual relationship. According to her testimony, when she asked him whether it was proper for them to be having sex, he "told me that when his medical class took the Hippocratic oath he was not present and it did not apply to him."

Clothing Optional

When officials of the American Dance Festival West in Salt Lake City decided not to censor nude performances but instead to warn patrons about the prospect of nudity, not one of the 350 people who had already bought tickets asked for a refund.

A naked man walked into a convenience store in Portland, Maine, during a snowstorm. Wielding a three-foot, double-edged sword that he raised and pointed at the store clerk's chest, he headed for the beer cooler. "I'm thirsty," the man told the clerk, according to police Lieutenant Nelson Bartley. As the clerk backed away and called the police, the naked customer left without taking anything. Bartley said police caught up with Michael L. Hicks, 29, a few blocks from the store, arrested him without a struggle, and warned him "not to go back to that address again—whether he has clothes on or not."

Police in Chatsworth, California, arrested Ilham Affane, 24, after she was found nude inside a church. Officers summoned by neighbors who reported hearing noises inside the church found Affane completely nude, jumping up and down on the pews, screaming, throwing Bibles around, and "generally acting in a bizarre manner," Los

Angeles Police Department spokesperson Mike Partain said.

Tina Rae Beavers, 19, was arrested in Great Falls, Montana, after she stretched out on the grass and exposed and fondled herself in full view of the jail where her husband, Ernie Beavers, was being held. Undersheriff John Strandell said Ernie Beavers had asked his wife for the show, although it was unclear whether he or other inmates actually saw Tina Beavers, who was charged with indecent exposure and unlawful communications with an inmate.

Brigita Volopichova, a 27-year-old district court judge in Pizen, Czechoslovakia, was disciplined for disgracing the legal profession after she appeared on television in Czechoslovakia's first "Miss Topless" contest. She came in second.

During the shooting of the movie *Stealing Beauty*, actress Liv Tyler, whose character was supposed to be posing for an artist, refused to bare both breasts, telling director Bernardo Bertolucci it would be "exploitative nudity." She insisted she would reveal only one breast.

Trailing the Western Baseball League in attendance, California's Palm Springs Suns announced plans for "Nude Night" at the ballpark, then had to cancel the promotion when it looked like attendance would exceed the stadium's 4,400-seat capacity. "So many people wanted to come, it could have filled Dodger Stadium," said the event's sponsor, Tom Mulhall, owner of a clothing-optional resort. "We were concerned that we might have a safety and security problem."

The Suns announced another promotion: "Priscilla, Queen of the Desert Suns Night." The event, named for an Australian cult movie, immediately ran afoul of the local gay community and was renamed "Female Impersonator Night." Even after the change, not everyone was happy. "I don't feel a baseball field is the place for a drag queen show," said hotelier Joe Riordan. "That's why you have nightclubs."

Police in Madison Township, Ohio, cited Kim Hansel, 37, for public indecency after someone complained she was mowing her lawn topless. She put bandages and leaves on her breasts and went back to mowing the lawn. Prosecutors dropped the indecency charge, but a judge fined Hansel $40 for disorderly conduct because she turned the riding mower around in the street after drinking.

When a Calcasieu Parish deputy stopped a 1990 Pontiac Grand Am on the main street of Vinton, Louisiana, a man got out, wearing only a towel. As the officer approached the car to find out what was going on, the man jumped back in and sped off. After a brief 90-miles-per-hour chase, the car hit a tree. Fifteen adults, as old as 63, piled out and began chanting religious sayings. Five children were in the trunk. "And they were completely nude. All twenty of them," said Police Chief Dennis Drouillard. "Didn't have a stitch of clothes on. I mean, no socks, no underwear, no nothing."

The driver, Sammy Rodriguez, 29, pastor of an Assembly of God church in Floydada, Texas, explained that God had warned him Judgment Day was at hand and to take his family and go to Florida to become evangelists. Along the way, they got rid of their clothes, believing them to be possessed by the devil. They also abandoned their money, pocketbooks, wallets, and other belongings.

Responding to a complaint from customers at a coin-operated laundry in Hancock, Michigan, police found a naked man playing an accordion while four friends danced partially naked as their clothes were washing. According to police Chief Mike Beaudoin, the man, a graduate student from Brazil, told officers, "I can't play the accordion unless I am completely nude."

When convicted burglar Tony Grimble, 40, appeared in court in Norwalk, California, to request a new trial, he wore "only an orange top with no bottoms," said Deputy District Attorney Diane Cressner. "I didn't look. I found it very offensive."

During the hour-long proceeding, Grimble spit on his lawyer, as well as Superior Court Judge Dewey Falcone (it was his first case), who never objected to Grimble's exposed genitals, although at one point he ordered Grimble shackled when he kept standing up and shouting, "Aliens! Aliens!"

Police in Bellevue, Washington, arrested a 65-year-old man for repeatedly exposing himself to a female newspaper carrier over a period of several weeks. A plainclothes female police officer arrested the man after she witnessed him standing naked in the front window of his home and later standing nude outside while brushing his teeth.

A man told police that his car was attacked by a naked red-haired woman as he drove alone at night along a dark country road near Wolverine, Michigan. The motorist, who described her as "the largest woman you ever saw," said she jumped out of the woods and came at the car.

Camden County, New Jersey, said it was considering spending $135,000 to frost the jail windows to discourage prisoners from posing nude or in various degrees of undress for friends and passers-by. In return, some people who gather in a parking lot across the street from the jail expose themselves to the inmates. "We have had the problem all day and night," Undersheriff William Cross said. "I have seen mothers out there in the parking lot at three o'clock in the morning, with infant babies."

When state police in Ogdensburg, New York, caught William J. Hess, 39, burglarizing a greenhouse, he was wearing nothing. He explained that he was naked so that anyone who saw him in the greenhouse couldn't identify him by describing his clothing.

Jeremiah Johnson, 18, arrived at a Florida court to answer a charge of driving without a license, but a bailiff told him he couldn't enter the courtroom wearing shorts. Johnson left briefly, then returned wearing nothing. Polk

County Judge Michael Raiden sentenced him to 179 days in jail for contempt of court.

Municipal officials in Cap d'Agde, the site of France's biggest international nudist colony, put up signs warning NUDITY OBLIGATORY and hired special police to ensure that people using the beach took off their clothes. Pointing out that extreme sunburn was the only exception, Mayor Gerard Paillou called the growing invasion of clothed vacationers "intolerable." He said more and more beach users are "simply refusing to get undressed."

The seven members of the Cap's beach patrol wear only white caps to identify themselves. One of them, identified by the newspaper *Liberation* only as Frederic, explained, "Every time we get someone to take their swimsuit off, we are happy and have the impression of playing a useful part in the life of the community."

Police in Davenport, Iowa, were notified of a man exposing himself on a busy city street by two women who spotted the 34-year-old suspect while driving by. The women explained that they felt it necessary to drive by again for a second look just to make sure.

Nudists from many European countries began flocking to Loch Lomond in Scotland. The *European* newspaper reported that nudists favored cold and damp Scotland because of fears over skin cancer from too much sun.

Sex and the Law

The Los Angeles Department of Building and Safety ordered an adult nightclub, the Odd Ball Cabaret, to close its main attraction: a shower enclosure where nude dancers performed for male customers. Officials explained that the enclosure had no wheelchair access, denying people in wheelchairs the opportunity to dance nude, even though none complained they were denied jobs because they couldn't get wheelchairs in the shower. Ron Shigeta, head of the department's Disabled Access Division, explained that the law is the law, no matter how ridiculous it might seem to some people.

Philadelphia's Department of Licenses and Inspections cited erotic dancer Crystal Storm after ascertaining that her bust measurement was only 50 inches, not the advertised "127." Storm explained that the figure was in centimeters, but department official Frank Antico declared, "That's deceptive advertising."

Commenting on the lack of sexual freedom in the United States, Austria's *Neue Zurcher Zeitung* reported that in Hastings, Nebraska, couples, married or not, are forbidden to sleep nude in hotel rooms. In Kentucky, a woman may appear on a state highway wearing a bathing suit only if two police officers are with her. In Tremonton, Utah, it is a crime for a woman to have sex with a man in an ambulance. An Alexandria, Minnesota, statute forbids men to engage in sex while their breath smells of garlic, onions, or sardines. And before the Olympic Games in Atlanta, the Georgia legislature debated whether to post lists of forbidden sexual practices in hotel rooms. The idea was dropped when one of the lawmakers pointed out that since many visitors to the Games would not be able to read English, the posted signs would have to rely on pictures and diagrams to make their point.

Malaysia's fundamentalist-Muslim Kelantan state ordered that the lights be left on in cinema halls during movies to prevent patrons from smooching. "We have directed lights to be switched on in cinemas during shows to prevent immoral acts like kissing, cuddling, and other activities," Kelantan Chief Minister Nik Aziz Nik Mat said. "If we can watch television at home with the lights on, then why not in cinemas?"

An inspection report filed by the Albuquerque Environmental Health Department warned that the Ice House, a nude dancing club, posed a sanitation risk. Noting that one of the acts at the club consisted of dancer Stephanie Evans expelling ping-pong balls from her vagina, the report pointed out that the balls could land on food or in drinks being consumed by club patrons.

British Labour Councilor Ben Summerskill accused undercover council officials and police of going "beyond the call of duty" after they visited a particular massage parlor 17 times. The inspectors, noting that they were given "amateurish massages" by scantily clad young women before being offered sex, which they politely refused, explained that the visits, which totaled $3,160, were necessary to prove that it was the owner and not the individual masseuses who were breaking the law.

When St. Paul, Minnesota, police arrested Johnny Koger on charges of soliciting sex from a prostitute, they confiscated his car under a city ordinance that lets cars be seized if they were used in the solicitation. After a jury found him not guilty, the city refused to return Koger's car until he paid a $1,100 storage free. Prosecutor Paul McCloskey justified the charge by explaining, "Just because a jury acquits, it doesn't say the man is innocent or that he's moral."

The mayor's office cited Koger's case as one more reason to "fine-tune" the ordinance. Another, it said, is that many johns who have their cars confiscated don't feel responsible about continuing to make payments, causing lenders to call the city attorney's office, trying to get their money.

Craig S. Johnson, 41, the mayor of Snow Hill, Maryland, was charged with misconduct for allowing a woman to pose naked on the top of a sheriff's squad car assigned to him. The mayor, who also worked as a deputy sheriff, reportedly contacted the operator of a pornographic Internet Web site and offered to help do the photos as a "prank," since he was leaving the sheriff's department. Local high school students found the pictures on the Web site.

During a debate by the North Carolina House Appropriations Committee on a state abortion fund for poor women, Representative Henry Aldridge, 71, tried to apologize for earlier remarks implying that victims of rape or incest are sexually promiscuous by expressing the belief that rape victims don't get pregnant. "The facts show that people who are raped—who are truly raped—the juices don't flow, the body functions don't work, and they don't get pregnant. Medical authorities agree this is a rarity, if ever."

Aldridge later defended his comments against criticism: "To get pregnant, it takes a little cooperation. And there ain't much cooperation with rape."

The Florida Supreme Court reprimanded Circuit Judge Leonard V. Wood, 61, for rude and inappropriate remarks he made to a divorcing couple, ordering Gary Lieberman and Julie Smith-Lieberman to disclose details of their sex life. After listening, he then urged them to stay married and have a baby, adding that he wouldn't mind fathering Smith-Lieberman's child himself if he wasn't already married.

Denver sheriff's officials unwittingly placed a 38-year-old female prisoner arrested on a prostitution charge in the men's jail, where she had consensual sex with two prisoners. Fifteen hours later, other prisoners tipped off deputies of 5-foot-7, 130-pound Jimmie Joe McGee's true gender. "I don't think this has ever happened before," Captain Carlos Jackson said, explaining that McGee's attitude toward being locked up with 60 men was "nonchalant."

*G*em County, Idaho, prosecutor Douglas Varie began using a little-known 75-year-old state law against fornication to try to wipe out teen pregnancy. "When I was first served with the papers, I didn't even know what fornication was," said a 17-year-old girl who received a 30-day suspended jail sentence and three years' probation. "It's an unmarried person who has sex, and they got me on that."

While fining Katie Nemeth, 19, who pleaded guilty to misusing a credit card by giving one she found to her boyfriend, Common Pleas Judge Shirley Strickland offered some advice: Dump your boyfriend, show your legs, and find a doctor to marry. "Men are easy," the Cleveland judge elaborated. "You can go to sit in the bus stop, put on a short skirt, cross your legs, and pick up 25. Ten of them will give you their money. If you don't pick up the first 10, then all you got to do is open your legs a little bit and cross them at the bottom and then they'll stop."

A Thai woman who was arrested on drug charges when police found amphetamines hidden in her underwear escaped when her interrogator passed out after consuming some 10 beers during a closed-door session. "It was not only beer that made the investigator exhausted," a police spokesperson said, "but they also had wild sex during the investigation."

Nevada lawmakers canceled a trip to tour the Mustang Ranch, a legal brothel near Reno, after a newspaper column ridiculed the plan. Assemblyman Bob Price, a Democrat from North Las Vegas, had called the trip a "fact-finding" mission to teach legislators about an industry that he says generates at least 30 percent of the tax revenue in some counties. But *Nevada Appeal* publisher and editor Jeff Ackerman ridiculed the tour, saying some taxpayers might suggest that "except for the degree of pleasure they provide, lawmakers and prostitutes might actually have lots in common."

Light slapping in a sadomasochistic relationship is not a legal offense as long as each partner agrees and is over the age of consent, a Belgian court ruled. It added, however, that the use of electric shocks, clamps, weights, and other such devices in sexual relationships still lays practitioners open to charges of lewd and lecherous behavior.

Chattanooga, Tennessee, Criminal Court Judge Doug Meyer released rape suspect Vincent L. Cousin after advising him to get a girlfriend. Violent men "must face why they hate women," Meyer explained, "and a girlfriend would help him do that." Three days later, after dozens of people complained about what he acknowledged were "ill-chosen words," the judge ordered Cousin taken into custody.

The Arizona Commission of Judicial Conduct reprimanded Magistrate Michael Lex for telling a woman prosecutor that "only whores wear red shoes." Brenda Cook, a Tucson assistant city prosecutor who filed the complaint, was wearing red shoes when Lex made the remark.

Redbook magazine named Allegheny County, Pennsylvania, Judge Robert P. Horgos one of "America's Most Sexist Judges" for asking a male attorney to take off his jacket, then inviting a female lawyer to "take off anything you want." Also named was Thomas Bollinger of Baltimore County, Maryland, who granted probation to a man convicted of raping a drunken woman, explaining that an unconscious woman on a bed was "the dream of a lot of males, quite honestly."

Terence Hadenham, 44, was convicted in Portsmouth, England, of gross indecency and indecent assault on a six-year-old girl. Rather than sentence Hadenham to jail, Judge John Whitley fined him $75 and gave him three years' probation. Whitley reasoned that Hadenham's stunted growth and a hearing impairment made it difficult for him to form relationships with women.

Convicted of cocaine possession, James Harris won a new trial after discovering that his attorney was carrying on an affair with one of the police officers who testified against him. Noting that court-appointed attorney Betty M. Hunter was involved in "a long-standing adulterous, intimate affair" with Marcello Muzzatti, one of the officers who searched Harris's Washington home, U.S. District Judge Royce Lamberth said that Hunter's cross-examination of Muzzatti at Harris's trial was "woefully inadequate," that the couple was seen leaving her home together just an hour after Harris was convicted, and that they vacationed together in the Bahamas between Harris's conviction and his sentencing.

Puerto Rico Senator Enrique Rodriguez Negron introduced a bill to create a Vasectomy Registry for men to notify when they have a vasectomy. Rodriguez explained that the measure would eliminate the popular custom of men facing paternity suits and demands for child support who have postdated vasectomies and profess sterility to show that they could not have fathered the children.

Former Colorado state Representative David Bath was convicted of charges stemming from an orgy that involved making a sexually exploitative videotape featuring a 17-year-old boy. Bath had cosponsored the law against the sexual exploitation of minors under which he was convicted.

After Gianfranco Napoleoni, 44, was convicted of attempting to rape his wife, Italy's Supreme Court overturned the conviction, accepting his claim that his action had been an effort to salvage the relationship.

A South Korean law aimed at cracking down on prostitution had to be rewritten after an appellate court in Seoul ruled that washing men's feet in barbershops is not an illegal sexual service.

Valery V. Karpov, a city councilor in Astrakhan, Russia, proposed that the city build a special youth hotel with hourly bedroom rates so young people who want to have sex don't have to use stairwells and cemeteries. When the proposal met a storm of protest from citizens accustomed to communist puritanism, Karpov responded, "What I proposed is nothing more than the sort of purpose motels in America are put to."

The University of Massachusetts at Amherst revised its Affirmative Action and Nondiscrimination Policy to include pedophiles—"persons whose sexual orientation includes minor children as the sex object"—as a protected minority.

The Dutch government ruled that prostitutes have to charge sales tax. Noting "that they are to be treated as entrepreneurs just as any other," Finance Ministry spokeswoman Mariette van Vucht explained that the law lets prostitutes deduct sales tax paid on job-related items, such as condoms and beds.

Police in Des Moines, Washington, hired Robert Berdue, 29, a convicted rapist, to have sex with suspected prostitutes. Despite Berdue's conviction, Police Chief Martin Pratt said that the department paid him to engage in sexual acts as an informant in a sting operation aimed at protecting the public interest from organized prostitution.

Judge Edward Kidd dismissed indecent exposure charges against a defendant in Roanoke, Virginia, general district court, despite testimony by a woman that he flashed her during a heated argument. The man explained that he could not have exposed himself since he had nothing to expose, a condition confirmed by an impromptu medical exam. Prosecutor Joel Branscom conceded, "I think it was one of the better defenses to an indecent exposure charge that I've ever seen."

Richard Redd, 46, the lawyer for the Baton Rouge, Louisiana, police department, was charged with malfeasance in office for asking exotic dancers and professional escorts to bare their breasts when they applied to him for the $25 licenses the city required for people in their line of work.

Sudhakar Rao Naik, chief minister of India's heavily populated Maharashtra state, proposed that jobs in government and public companies be denied to parents with more than two children. To control India's burgeoning population, Naik also recommended that anyone in elected office who has a third child be forced to resign.

In approving an anti-nudity ordinance, the Kenosha, Wisconsin, city council nixed an amendment that would have banned "covered male genitals in a discernibly turgid state," meaning that men could have been arrested for becoming sexually aroused while fully clothed.

Clinicas de Salud Del Pueblo, Inc., a medical company in Brawley, California, announced that workers who display hickeys would be sent home without pay. They may return when the telltale marks of passion disappear or are covered up, personnel manager Diana Tamex said, explaining that the company implemented the rule in response to complaints from colleagues and patients at the company's three health care clinics.

According to Dr. Mark Goulston, assistant clinical professor of psychiatry at UCLA, the small marks can lead to large fantasies. "Someone with a low sex drive may look at it as a bruise," he said. "Someone with a lot of sex on their mind will look at a hickey as if they're watching Sharon Stone in *Basic Instinct*."

Harrison, Arkansas, Municipal Judge Don West found defendant Melissa Thurston in contempt for not wearing a bra in court, calling her attire "offensive." "I was wearing a high-neck sweater," Thurston explained. "It wasn't see-through or anything. He had to be staring right at me."

Minnesota's Moorhead State University banned mistletoe after psychology professor Margaret Potter filed a grievance saying it encourages sexual harassment.

In Maine, U.S. District Judge D. Brock Hornby ruled against Penobscot County Jail inmate Juanita Crosby Williams, who filed a $100,000 suit claiming her constitutional right to privacy was violated when she was placed in the same cell with Cheyenne Deneuve Lamson, also known as Roger Miles Jr., a preoperative male transsexual. Hornby said jail officials who decided, on sound medical advice, that Lamson was a woman acted reasonably when "confronted with a situation that had no perfect answer."

Health officials in Caroline County, Maryland, reported success with their program to curb teenage pregnancies by paying girls ages 12 to 17 who already have had a baby a dollar a day not to get pregnant again. Of the 12 girls who signed up in the first year, only one became pregnant.

Wisconsin, meanwhile, resumed paying teenage parents from $447 to $517 a month if they got married. Under the program championed by Governor Tommy Thompson and dubbed "Bridefare" by critics, the money is added to couples' welfare checks.

A court in Peterborough, Ontario, ordered the eviction of a 25-year-old female college student from her two-bedroom apartment because of her loud lovemaking. "The major complaint," said the judge, "is that the moaning during lovemaking is so loud it disturbs other tenants."

The family living below her moved out over the behavior. Another tenant said "the moaning" occurred several nights a week, often twice and sometimes three times each evening, with each incident "lasting half an hour to an hour." The building superintendent said that when the defendant's windows were open, "you could hear her a block away." He also commented on her "steady stream of boyfriends," clarifying, "I don't think it was a business with her. I think it was a problem."

For her part, the student blamed all the fuss on poor building insulation.

A judge in Jay, New York, found a snow sculptor guilty of obscenity for building a snow scene of a female snow figure performing oral sex on a male snow figure. The judge fined the sculptor $500 and ordered a state police officer to destroy the snow figures.

A judge in Genoa, Italy, acquitted a 20-year-old girl of nude sunbathing along a riverbank "because the fact does not constitute a crime," but at the same time convicted the woman's three male friends of committing obscene acts in public. According to the judge, "The male anatomical conformation can become obscene even unconsciously."

The Texas Supreme Court ruled that the beneficiaries of a 33-year-old male victim who died during autoerotic sex were entitled to collect accidental death benefits, affirming a lower court ruling that the victim's hanging death was accidental. "Aside from his propensity to unusual sexual practices," the court explained, "[the man] was a well-adjusted, happy individual who was looking forward to the future and did not intend to commit suicide."

According to the court record the victim waited for his wife to go shopping and then dressed in her underwear and wig and tied a nylon rope around his neck, looping it over a bedroom door and securing it to the doorknob on the opposite side of the door. Then through a pulley system the man was able to use the pressure of his foot to tighten the noose, decreasing his oxygen supply, intending to heighten the sexual pleasure of masturbation. A coroner ruled that his foot must have slipped, putting his full weight on the rope and hanging himself.

Prison inmates at St. Albans State Prison in Vermont who participated in a "victim empathy class" were forced to withstand simulated anal rape while a therapist shouted obscenities at them. Prison authorities said that the "drama therapy" was intended to teach the inmates, all of whom were convicted rapists, what their victims had experienced. The American Civil Liberties Union filed suit on behalf of the inmates, seeking a halt to the program, saying that it "traumatized, sickened and terrified" the inmates.

Police in Lynnwood, Washington, were assigned to a local hotel to assure that the 1990 Mr. Male beauty contest did not violate a city ordinance that forbids topless adult entertainment. "They've got their nipples covered," said a police spokesman of the contestants, who were dressed only in bikini briefs and small pieces of flesh-colored tape over their nipples. A state Liquor Control Board agent also attended the contest to make sure that there was at least six feet of space between contestants and the audience.

Eat It

Dean Ludwig Bee, 30, told police in Harrisville, West Virginia, that he had been drinking at a bar when he accepted a ride home from another man whom he did not know. Bee said that he fell asleep in the man's car and awoke in a strange house, where he found the man licking condiments off his naked body. "There was ketchup, mustard, mayonnaise, pickles—things out of the refrigerator. Different types of food were all over me," he said. "I went crazy." He admitted stabbing the man, a local funeral director, 13 times.

A 21-year-old Warren, Ohio, woman awoke to the sound of burglars leaving her home only to discover that they had covered her buttocks with whipped cream and sugar.

A restaurant owner in Livermore, California, lost a $45,000 sexual harassment suit filed by four waitresses who were offended that he served hamburgers shaped like male genitalia.

After Egyptian columnist Farag Fouda ridiculed a militant Islamic group for having banned eggplants and squash because of their supposed sexual connotations, two men on a motorcycle gunned him down.

The Australian Federation of AIDS organizations announced it was seeking donations of used dildos to replace carrots and bananas being used in sex education programs in developing nations. Sponsors admitted that produce wasn't getting the point across.

Britain's Vegetarian Society launched a new advertising campaign in movie theaters portraying vegetables as sex objects. The 40-second spots, which the group made to spice up vegetables' boring image, involve suggestively shaped chilies, melon fondling, and a flaccid asparagus. "We tried to avoid the real clichés like cucumbers and eggplants," said the organization's head of public affairs, Chris Dessent, who added the spots have no cauliflower. "Just couldn't make cauliflower sexy. We succeeded with a pea, though. We shot a male hand gently tickling one."

Twins Magazine announced it was surveying its readers to see if there was a connection between yams and multiple births. The research was triggered by studies of the Nigerian Yoruba tribe, which has four times the multiple births of the United States and eats lots of yams.

Sandra McRae filed a lawsuit against the owner of a Dunkin' Donuts shop in Nashua, New Hampshire, complaining that the store sold her a dozen fried doughnut holes shaped like "a male sex organ, complete with testes." She said she suffered emotional distress when she opened the box for some coworkers, who saw the

Munchkins peering up at them. "There was no doubt about what it was," she declared.

Nestlé Canada, Inc., announced a change in label design for its Zoodles brand of noodles after a 42-year-old Nova Scotia woman complained that when the can was turned upside down, the cartoon palm trees resembled penises.

A former U.S. Customs agent in Houston, Texas, was sentenced to seven years' probation for promoting prostitution. Among the women he touted were the city's infamous "Salad Sisters," named for acts they performed, on each other and their clients, with fruits and vegetables.

Sex for Hire

*G*rowing intolerance of sexual harassment in the Japanese workplace prompted several Tokyo strip clubs to re-create office settings where men can fondle women dressed in working clothes.

*O*fficers at Sweden's Karlberg military academy gave cadets a lesson in discipline by hiring a whip-wielding dominatrix to entertain them. One cadet reported, "It wasn't particularly pleasant."

*T*yler Green of Gahanna, Ohio, filed a lawsuit against adult film star Amber Lynn, claiming he was injured when she fell on him. According to Green's suit, he made the winning bid during an auction, entitling him to watch Lynn dance above him and remove her underwear. He was told to lie on his back, then Lynn began dancing over him "and then without warning from a standing position, dropped and/or jumped upon the Plaintiff's chest, buttocks first, causing the Plaintiff to feel excruciating pain in his rib area and gasp for breath." Attorney Barrett McInerney, representing Amber Lynn Productions International, disputed the account, explaining that Green "purchased the right to get where he was, and then decided—instead of keeping his hands at his side—to reach up and try to drag her down, and she lost her balance." In either case, McInerney noted that Lynn weighs about 125 pounds and "doesn't exactly play offensive lineman."

A Swedish court convicted a 34-year-old taxi driver of overcharging a 49-year-old woman after he left the meter running while he had sex with her. According to the *Aftonbladet* newspaper, the driver billed the woman the equivalent of $8,300 for 25 occasions of "sexual services." The bill included 25 percent sales tax, plus charges for trips, hotel, and telephone calls. A district court ruled the driver had exploited the woman's longing for physical love.

When Broward County, Florida, enacted a new ordinance governing X-rated entertainment, two adult businesses owned by Michael Rogers stopped their nude strip shows, changed their names, and offered different services. The first, Club Romance, provided men with female dance partners, who, Rogers said, "got all their clothes on and just sit and talk to guys."

The other business, Secretaries Are Us, offered women who let men indulge in verbal sexual harassment for $50 a half hour. Rogers said customers get to sit behind a desk and say whatever they want to a woman, explaining, "You can speak freely to a secretary without opening yourself up to a lawsuit." He added: "I know I can make money without someone taking their clothes off."

Danish officials approved providing help for disabled clients visiting prostitutes, explaining that in some cities social workers would escort the person to a massage parlor for a 30-minute visit costing about $100. Although the government will pay for the social workers, the customers must pay for the visit.

After jailing the members of two prostitution rings, police in Xiangzhou, China, reported that all the women were over 70 years old, and the oldest was 93. "This is not just a moral issue," a spokesperson from the vice squad explained. "More seriously, these people are clearly contravening the terms of their pension by continuing to work."

The women reportedly worked in the city's central Fengboshan Park, serving 200 clients a month. Pleasures included nude peeking (costing 5 yuan), bosom touching (10 yuan), and oral sex (60 yuan, rising to 80 yuan if the client wanted the woman to remove her teeth).

In Natal, Brazil, Madam Maria Oliveira Barros, 74, closed her brothel and sold it and the land it was on for $562,000. However, five of her former prostitute employees announced that they were suing their former madam for $112,000, which they claim will cover their unpaid holidays and unpaid overtime compensation for working nights. One of the five worked there for 17 years.

Firefighters searching a hotel in Cologne during a major fire found a man, identified by German law enforcement authorities as a very wealthy "senior German business executive," tied spread-eagled to the bed and gagged. They said he had hired a 28-year-old dominatrix for the evening, but when she heard the guest in the suite next door screaming fire, she ran out on her client.

Police in King County, Washington, arrested a couple who founded the Ultimate Life Church near Puget Sound, charging them with promoting prostitution. The church advocated hug ceremonies and closeness, but police charged that it was all just a front for a major prostitution ring. One police spokesman said that the church looked "exactly like a massage parlor. There's a reception area and two rooms where 'communion' is held." Parishioners paid dues or donations of $50 or $60 and participated in a "baptism of pleasure" administered by a female minister.

Germany's minister of women, Christine Bergmann, announced that she would submit a bill calling for health, retirement, and unemployment benefits for prostitutes. The measure would also give the women a legal right to sue customers who refuse to pay for their services. Bergmann added that prostitutes should be able to retire, with full benefits, by age 60.

Amsterdam's Nude Cleaning Services began charging Dutch homemakers $43 an hour for a naked man to come to their house to clean and do the laundry. The business soon was taking some 40 orders a day, according to founder Edgar van Wingerden. "Some more elderly women, especially, like to see a scantily clad young man about the place, doing the work," he said. "Many of the single people who call us in are just in need of social contact. Often very little cleaning gets done."

In Iran, where prostitution is illegal, men can register with a religious court for an "enjoyment marriage," which lasts 10 minutes. The London *Observer* reported that a general's widow who recently published her memoirs claimed to have had hundreds of such temporary husbands in the past 20 years, including "one ayatollah, 21 senior clergymen, five famous merchants, a few hundred university students, and the head of a hospital."

After a man in Stockholm, Sweden, telephoned a prostitute, arranged to meet her, and then didn't show up, the prostitute submitted a $200 bill. When he didn't pay, she sued. Since prostitution is legal in Sweden, the woman insisted she has the same right to collect debts as other business people. "If a dentist makes an appointment with a customer and that person chooses not to show up at the agreed-upon time and place," she said, "then he or she would be charged for the visit."

Germany's Romeo Cleaners introduced a new service intended for Berliners who had become jaded with Christmas: decorating Christmas trees while naked. "Since we opened a year ago, we have had a thriving service in men and women cleaning people's houses with no clothes on," Romeo's director, Ralk Knuth, said. "But people demanded something new and even more quirky." Noting that the service cost $64 for an afternoon, Knuth explained, "Staff arrive in fancy dress, which can range from Superman to traditional transvestite attire. Items of clothing are removed as the afternoon progresses."

Rick's Cabaret International Inc. announced plans to become the first topless bar traded on Wall Street by applying for a listing on the Nasdaq exchange. The Houston nightspot said it expected its stock offering to raise $4.9 million to expand to other cities.

Lyle Craig Bain, a former alderman in New London, Wisconsin, was sentenced to 120 days in jail for trying to solicit women to pay him for sex.

Felicia Miles, 30, lost custody of her son in Rockford, Illinois, after she admitted hiring a dancer for his twelfth birthday party who stripped down to a halter and G-string. Miles said she allowed her son to lick whipped cream off the dancer's breasts.

A dollar-a-chance raffle aimed at raising money to help surfer Trudy Todd, 18, of Queensland, Australia, continue competing on the world professional surfing circuit offered as first prize a date with a prostitute. Todd's parents approved the fund-raiser when a prostitute offered her services after Todd's father rescued her from a male attacker.

Dutch prostitutes were invited to join Prosex, an off-shoot of the country's main trade union, to improve their working conditions, stop exploitation, and set standards of service. Sadomasochistic sessions, for example, would be more strictly regulated. The mistress must guarantee client safety, keep a key nearby, and ensure that hand-cuffs and other bindings take no longer than 30 seconds to unfasten in case of an emergency.

Australia's brothels and sex shops announced a boycott of French-made adult videos, magazines, and sex toys to protest President Jacques Chirac's decision to resume nuclear testing in the South Pacific. "French-maid outfits and French knickers are being taken out of window dis-plays and requests for condoms as French letters are to be ignored," said the Eros Foundation, which represents Australia's sex trade. "The industry is also undertaking a major review of language and terminology which paints the French as lovers and therefore peaceful."

Scantily clad entertainers were banned in Jakarta on New Year's Eve. Nightclubs in the Indonesian capital regularly feature foreign musicians and dancers, some of them erot-ic, but a spokesperson for the head supervisor of foreign artists at City Hall said such bawdy revelry is not appropri-ate during the holy month of Ramadan, warning, "We will bring down any foreign artist who wears a bikini on stage."

Female prostitutes in the sleazy market area of down-town Mexico City won the right to ply their trade by agreeing to wear sensible clothes and behave nicely. In an accord signed with city authorities, the hookers promised not to wear skirts more than four fingers above the knee or see-through clothing before 10 p.m. Other concessions include no soliciting near schools and churches, strict hours of business, no drinking on the street or bad language, and only women allowed. In exchange, city officials agreed that the prostitutes could work on designated streets.

A Hong Kong court sentenced Chan Wing-hong, 38, to five years in jail after he admitted killing and dismembering the only woman he ever loved because she called him a dwarf. The 4-foot-6 Chan said he spent all his money during the five-week relationship with the prostitute because she was his "first girlfriend." The couple argued when Chan ran out of money. "She said, 'You bloody dwarf. I see no reason I like you,' " Chan said. "I was very disappointed."

When Tammy Papler, the owner of the New Life Massage Parlor in Oak Grove, Kentucky, accused city officials and police of taking bribes to allow her to run her business as a brothel and of buying sex from her girls, city councilor Patty Belew backed up Papler's allegations. Belew admitted that she worked as a prostitute at Papler's massage parlor for about two years. When some of the town's 3,000 residents called for her to resign from the council, Belew said she was remaining in office because "there ain't nobody else in there that's any better than I am. At least I did come out and tell the truth, unlike everybody else."

At a professional development workshop in Utrecht, Dutch prostitutes were counseled on how to make the most of their job. The four-day course covered health, crisis management, and job satisfaction. "There are 35,000 women working in the Dutch relaxation industry, and many suffer from low self-esteem," Henk Klein Beekman of the relaxation industry employers' union said, explaining that prostitution is "more than just sex. It's dealing with men's feelings, and it can be fun."

When Thai reporters asked Bangkok's chief of police, Viroj Pao-in, if his officers were taking bribes from brothel owners, he said that was impossible because brothels do not exist in the Thai capital. The next day, Crime Division Commander Rangsit Yanothai told reporters, "There are numerous brothels in Bangkok." When reminded of his chief's remarks, he quickly withdrew his comment.

The Australian government ordered a brothel in South Australia to set up a training program for its employees or pay penalties. Under Australian law, any firm with sales over a certain amount must spend one percent of the total on training.

Italian prostitutes in Biella began offering free samples to lure customers away from immigrants, whom they accused of undercutting set prices.

An alternate juror on an investigating grand jury in Delaware County, Pennsylvania, was dismissed after he hired a male stripper to put on a surprise performance at the county courthouse to celebrate a female grand juror's birthday. The unidentified juror said he had planned to have the stripper perform at a nearby restaurant but changed plans because heavy rain kept the jurors from going out to lunch.

The day after Hungary's parliament swore in the nation's first post-Communist government, Budapest business-man Laszlo Voros announced plans to turn the capital into the Bangkok of Eastern Europe by opening brothels and massage parlors and operating sex taxis, sex boats, and a sex bus. He noted: "Human rights and democracy express themselves in the field of sexuality as well."

An ad in the *Detroit Free Press* noted that the club Deja Vu has "25 Beautiful Showgirls" and "3 Ugly Ones."

Canada's Conservative government admitted that its Federal Business Development Bank helped finance Le Lido, a flourishing strip club in Hull, Quebec, across the river from Ottawa. Employing some 20 female exotic dancers, the bar, located near a federal office complex, was well known as an afternoon haunt for civil servants. "They have lots of money for the girls and they drink a fair bit," owner André Frechette said. "I guess they have bor-ing jobs."

Fruits of Research

Sex began 1.1 billion years ago, scientists announced after concluding that's when single-cell plankton developed pores that allowed sex cells to be released into the ocean. Citing diversity among plankton fossils that they analyzed, paleobiologists J. William Schopf of the University of California at Los Angeles and Carl Mendelson of Beloit College in Wisconsin noted that until the origin of sexual reproduction, which combined characteristics of both parents, asexually begotten offspring were genetic copies of previous generations.

Vigorous sex can cause blurred vision, according to Johns Hopkins University researchers. The temporary condition, called Valsava retinopathy, usually is associated with other forms of exertion, such as weightlifting, or with prolonged vomiting or severe coughing. It results from tiny blood vessels breaking or delicate tissue at the back of the eyeball tearing. Dr. Neil M. Bressler, a coauthor of the study, commented, "Maybe this gives us a physical explanation as to why there were some old wives' tales that certain sexual activities could result in blindness."

There is no sex in heaven, Pope John Paul II proclaimed while visiting a parish in Rome. Residents don't miss it, he explained, because "they are like the angels."

Sponsors of California's San Jose Auto Show hastily withdrew their offer to Cindy Crawford of "between $50,000 and $100,000" for a two-day appearance after reading a poll in the current issue of *Men's Journal* magazine. It revealed that 86 percent of the respondents would rather receive a new Land Rover than go on a date with the model. Noting that a Land Rover Discovery cost $35,000, publicist Peter Ciccarelli explained, "We were offering this exorbitant amount of money to Cindy Crawford when we could just put a Land Rover on display."

Women get a surge of the male hormone testosterone after they drink alcohol, according to a new study, which suggested that the increase may help explain why drinking can arouse women sexually. Researchers reporting in the journal *Nature* said that alcohol's effect on testosterone was strongest in women who were taking oral contraceptives. Alcohol did not increase testosterone in men, the researchers concluded, leaving them unable to explain why drinking makes men sexually excited.

Among preschoolers, only 30 percent of boys and 21 percent of girls know the proper words for their genitals, according to researchers at Case Western Reserve

University medical school who interviewed mothers of children ages 1 to 4.

The prevalence of female nudity in films offends two-thirds of the 2,000 women surveyed by *Glamour* magazine, but 86 percent said that there should be more male nudity on-screen.

Sex is less dangerous to the heart than getting out of bed, according to a study of men and women recovering from heart attacks. Dr. James Muller found that only one percent of the subjects' heart attacks were triggered by sexual activity, whereas 10 percent were triggered by awakening abruptly. Muller added that a healthy 50-year-old man faces a one-in-a-million risk of a heart attack; after sex, he faces a two-in-a-million risk.

People with sexual disorders often use their cars to appease their compulsions, posing a danger to others, according to psychologists. Helen Friedman, a clinical psychologist in St. Louis who deals with sex addicts, said some of her clients have had accidents because they've been so preoccupied with sexual fantasies. The triggers for the fantasies might have been a casual glance from another driver or the sight of a woman walking down the street, she said, explaining, "Things that for you and me would be no big deal can set some people off."

British women prefer dining out to making love, according to a survey by *Good Housekeeping* magazine.

The scent of a woman's sweat acts as an aphrodisiac, according to a report in *Physician's Weekly*. Researchers collected women's sweat, froze it for a year, then rubbed it periodically on the lips of 11 women. They reported increased sexual activity.

Researchers at the University of Utah in Salt Lake City announced they have discovered a link between high-fat foods such as burgers, fries, and milkshakes and the male sex drive. In their study involving eight men, eating fatty foods lowered their testosterone production by 30 percent.

Public transportation ranks among the top 10 ways to meet a mate, according to a survey conducted for Korbel Champagne Cellars Department of Romance, Weddings & Entertaining.

Twenty percent of French women, according to a survey reported in the newsmagazine *Le Point*, do not think an interviewer should be censured for asking a job applicant to disrobe.

Kissing represents one of the most intensive uses of muscles in the body, according to plastic surgeons at the Phoenix Research Unit at London's University College. By placing electrodes over the lips and cheeks of volunteers, they determined that kissing involves almost every muscle and that one passionate session of lip aerobics could burn 150 calories—about the same as 15 minutes of swimming laps.

Several ultra-Orthodox rabbis in Israel banned the use of a "purity computer" to determine when people may have sex. The handheld device helps couples comply with Jewish law, which forbids sex from 12 hours before menstruation starts to seven days after it ends. Instead of turning to rabbis for help with the calculation, the woman need only enter information about her menstrual cycle to learn when sex is permissible. Rabbi Yosef Halevi Eliashiv, an authority on Jewish law, warned that the "purity computer" might just be the start of technology's taking over rabbis' traditional authority.

In-flight sex is on the rise, according to *The Wall Street Journal*, which reported that one-third of the cases of "unruly behavior" aboard Singapore Airlines involved sexual misconduct. South African Airways reported that on one of its flights from Johannesburg to London, "a couple in business class disrobed from the waist down and began having sex in a seat in full view of other passengers." They stopped only when the captain stepped into the passenger cabin and yelled at them that his airplane was "not a shag house."

Smoking could reduce the size of a man's erect penis, according to researchers at the Boston University School of Medicine. Their study concluded that smoking affects the penis much as it does the heart, damaging the blood vessels and inhibiting blood flow, which in turn affects elastin, the substance believed to govern a man's ability to have an erection.

Russians and Americans have sex more than twice as often as the Spanish, according to a survey by the makers of Durex condoms. The poll of 10,000 sexually active adults in 15 countries found that Russians had sexual intercourse an average of 135 times a year and Americans 133 times. Thais had sex 71 times a year and Spaniards 64 times. Singaporeans make love an average of 89 times a year, compared with 77 times for Hong Kong citizens and 67 times for Malaysians. The French topped the list with 168 times. The global average is 119 times.

São Paulo cardiovascular surgeon Roberto Tullii announced that stress, caused by the poor economy, accounts for the sexual problems of 60 percent of men seeking his services, twice the number 10 years earlier. Their average age also has fallen to 37 from 47 in 1986, when Brazil began a series of austere, anti-inflation programs. Tullii told *Estado de São Paulo* that professional males are most at risk from stress-related sexual problems, explaining, "It would be hard to find a shoe shiner suffering from impotence."

Nearly half the Germans surveyed by the Emnid Institute said network television doesn't show enough pornography. Networks already air graphic movies and sex-talk shows late at night, but 48 percent of the viewers surveyed said they would like to see more porn.

According to *TV Today* magazine, which commissioned the survey, "The last taboo has fallen."

Americans with college degrees have sex less than those who only finished high school, according to a 10-year study by the National Opinion Research Center at the University of Chicago. The survey, reported in *American Demographics* magazine, also noted that people who went to graduate school are the least sexually active educational group. It also found that people who said they had the least free time, especially those working at least 65 hours a week, have the most sex. What's more, about 15 percent of adults have half of all the sex. Finally, the most sexually active Americans are jazz fans, gun owners, and people who lack confidence in the president.

Women who wear provocative attire may devote so much mental activity to their appearance that their brains aren't able to think of much else, according to University of Michigan psychologist Barbara Frederickson. "It isn't just clothes like bathing suits, that are revealing or low-cut, that can have this effect," Frederickson said. "Any clothing or circumstances that make a woman feel self-conscious about how she looks to others, even if she thinks she looks great, might reduce the mental energy she brings to demanding tasks, like solving advanced math problems."

Researchers at the University of Wisconsin reported in the *Journal of Family Psychology* that married couples in dual-income households have sexual relations almost as often (5.63 times a month) as couples where the woman stays home (5.96 times).

Hot-blooded Greek lovers who sweep foreign women off their feet are a thing of the past, according to that country's Sexological Institute, which reported that Greek men between 20 and 35 have neither the time nor the desire to enjoy sex. They're so obsessed with their jobs, in fact, that they aren't even inclined to fantasize about sex. "To discover that Greeks have much less sex than was widely believed was indeed surprising," said Dr. Zisis Papathanasiou, a gynecologist who headed the survey, adding that the demands of women are as much to blame as the anxiety caused by work and role models. "Many men said they found women too demanding, both sexually and emotionally. They were particularly disturbed when women took the sexual initiative."

Scientists at the Ethyl Corporation in Baton Rouge, Louisiana, announced they had developed Zeolite A, a substance that makes roosters more sexually aggressive. The researchers disclosed that they tested the substance by counting the number of times the roosters jumped on graduate student volunteers.

Men's Fitness magazine cited studies conducted in California that found married men who quit smoking cigarettes and cigars have twice as much sex as smokers.

A statistical study of villagers in Caerphilly, Wales, found that men who have more sex seem to live longer and that having regular sex reduces the risk of death by about half. Reporting their findings in *The British Medical Journal*, the researchers, headed by Dr. George Davey-Smith, suggested that their findings might inspire a campaign to promote the benefits of an active sex life.

A pocket-size device called the "Discovery I" was developed in Taiwan to detect hidden cameras used by pornographers to videotape unsuspecting couples having sex and women trying on clothes. The videos are staples of the country's underground porn market. The device works by detecting radio waves emitted by the remote-controlled cameras that the pornographers commonly install in hotel rooms, public toilets, and department store fitting rooms.

Circumcised men experience a wider variety of sexual practices than uncircumcised men, according to University of Chicago researchers. Writing in the *Journal of the American Medical Association*, they reported that besides being more likely to engage in oral and anal sex, circumcised men also masturbate more frequently. That finding is particularly interesting, the researchers noted, because circumcision was once widely advocated to prevent masturbation.

Dutch doctors announced the development of a new surgical technique "to reconstruct the hymens of adolescent

girls who are no longer virgins but wish to appear so."
Rotterdam gynecologist Adrian Logsman reported in the
British Medical Journal that the operations are intended
chiefly for "immigrant women" from cultures that require
brides to be virgins.

According to a survey taken by Black Pearl Records of
New Jersey:

- "Single women who earned over $45,000 a year were 79
  percent less likely to listen to music during sex than
  married women who earned over $45,000 a year."
- "Twelve percent of single women who listen to jazz during sex professed to wanting abortion banned."
- "Seventeen percent of married women who listen to
  alternative music also enjoyed watching porno movies
  after returning home from a music concert, while 24
  percent of single women who listen to rhythm and
  blues music preferred having sex before going out on a
  date."
- "Fifty-six percent of married women said they enjoyed
  a sporting event more if a well-known male singer sang
  the national anthem before the game."
- "Sixty percent of women who listen to Luther Vandross
  professed that kissing was more important than sex."

Women who have breast enlargements tend to drink
more, have more sex partners, get pregnant younger, and
dye their hair more than other women, according to cancer researcher Linda S. Cook. She said her study suggests
implants could be getting unfair blame for health problems that might really be caused by lifestyle factors.

Of 555 married couples asked "Would you rather have OK sex in a clean house or great sex in a dirty house?" for James Thornton's book, *Chore Wars: How Households Can Share the Work and Keep the Peace*, 31 percent of the women and 31 percent of the men said they wanted great sex in a dirty house. But 53 percent of the women and 56 percent of the men chose OK sex in a clean house.

A University of Michigan survey found that marital bliss peaks during the honeymoon, declines for the next 20 years, but then soars to new heights around the thirty-fifth anniversary. "Our results show that declines in work and parental responsibilities explain a large portion of the increase in marital satisfaction in the later years of marriage," UM sociologist Terri L. Orbuch said. "Declining income and increasing assets in later life also explain a small portion of the increase."

The Andrology Institute, a private reproductive firm in Lexington, Kentucky, reported that its survey determined the time when most people are likely to be having sex is 10:34 P.M.

Glamour magazine announced the best month to have sex is October, explaining, it's "the annual peak of testosterone in men."

Indiana University researcher Jeff Alberts reported his studies show that astronauts should avoid having sex in outer space or at least practice birth control. Alberts put 10 pregnant rats aboard space shuttle flights, then studied what happened to the mothers and babies after they returned to Earth. He discovered the mothers were lethargic, flexed their muscles less, and let their tails droop. When they gave birth, they required twice as many muscle contractions as normal to deliver their babies. The babies' eyes and inner ears were abnormal and mis-shapen, and they were unable to tell up from down when swimming. "I wouldn't want to be pregnant in space," Alberts said. "At least not until we learn a lot more about the process."

The National Sex Health Survey, conducted by researcher Joseph Catania of the University of California at San Francisco, found no difference in rates of use of sex toys in urban and nonfarm rural areas (10 percent). The survey did note that use in farm areas was only 7 percent.

Marital infidelity has become more tolerable to Canadians, according to a CTV/Angus Reid poll, which found that 51 percent of Canadians considered cheating more socially acceptable than it was 10 years ago. Almost two in 10 Canadians admitted to having had an extramarital affair.

The future of sex, according to social scientist Joel Snell, is robots. Writing in the journal *The Futurist*, Snell predicted the sexbot could be individually programmed for personalized pleasure and eventually "robotic sex may become 'better' than human sex. They will be disease-free; they won't judge one's sexual performance, and they won't say no." Best of all, Snell reported: "Prototype models have already been imported from Japan."

The fabled French sex drive is waning, according to a survey for the magazine *L'Evenement du Jeudi*, which found that 38 percent of those polled make love less frequently than they used to. Only 9 percent said they have more sex than before. Forty-nine percent said they often or sometimes have no desire to make love; what's more, 52 percent said they would not be bothered by going without sex for long periods.

In a survey by the British condom maker Durex, 57 percent of the American women responding and 42 percent of the men said that an unlimited shopping spree on someone else's gold credit card appealed to them more than sex.

The European maker of Pergonal blamed a shortage of the popular fertility drug on unanticipated demand. Pergonal, produced in Switzerland by Laboratories Serono SA and used by 30 percent to 50 percent of infertile couples undergoing treatment, is made from the urine of postmenopausal women. Noting that the shortage threatened to halt infertility procedures throughout the United States, the *Hartford Courant* reported that when Pergonal was introduced in the 1960s, Serono's source for postmenopausal urine was a convent near its Rome headquarters. Today, Serono collects urine twice a day from more than 100,000 European donors.

A baby girl was born in England to a surrogate mother almost five years after she was conceived. Newborn Jennifer Gunther spent the time as a frozen embryo while her biological parents searched for a suitable surrogate in which to implant the embryo. They found one four years and two months later. Under British laws, embryos frozen after 1991 must be destroyed after five years.

An Italian woman whose eggs were fertilized and then frozen died six months later in a car crash. Gynecologist Pasquale Bilotta told the Italian news agency ANSA that soon after the accident, the woman's husband asked him to implant the embryos in his sister. The sister gave birth to a baby girl, Elisabetta, born two years after her biological mother's death.

Also in Italy, after she and her husband tried to adopt a baby but were turned down because of their age, 62-year-old Rosanna Della Corte gave birth to a baby boy. According to gynecologist Severino Antinori, whose clinic arranged the artificial insemination of Della Corte with her husband's sperm and a donor's egg, the world's oldest mother had hormone treatments that give her "the physique of a 30-to-45-year-old. Her son won't be growing up with an old woman, but with a woman who is like 35."

James Austin, a 26-year-old unmarried bank analyst, paid an Indianapolis infertility clinic $30,000 to arrange for a surrogate mother to bear his child. Five weeks after his son's birth, Austin was charged with killing the baby by repeatedly beating and shaking him. Austin's attorney suggested that the clinic was responsible for the baby's murder because it failed to prepare Austin for fatherhood.

The World Health Organization reported that people have sex at least a hundred million times a day. "I think it might be an underestimation," admitted Dr. Mahmoud Fathalla, author of the WHO report, who computed the figure by multiplying the world birth rate by the accepted estimate of the number of times sex does not result in conception. "It is not the outcome of a survey we have carried out worldwide to find out how much fun is going on in the world."

Too much sex can be sickening, according to government researchers, who used laboratory animals to discover that sexual activity suppresses the body's immune system and reduces its ability to fend off disease-causing organisms. "The animals that engaged in sex until they reached the point of satiety were most profoundly affected," said Dr. Nancy Ostrowski, a National Institute of Mental Health researcher who headed up the work. "On the other hand, even minimal first-time exposure to sex was sufficient to suppress parts of the immune system."

After analyzing 758 sayings attributed to Jesus and judging only 148 to be authentic, a committee of religious scholars, led by Robert W. Funk of California's Westar Institute, declared that Jesus was probably not celibate, did not advocate celibacy, and had a "special relationship" with at least one woman.

Eleven percent of Americans would rather iron their clothes in the morning than have sex, according to a 1990 poll reported in *Men's Health* magazine.

A new medical procedure was developed to help paraplegic men become fathers. Called "electroejaculation," it stimulates damaged nerves by delivering a 10-volt electrical charge via a rectal probe to the prostate and seminal vesicles, causing ejaculation. Doctors collect the semen and inseminate the wife. Despite the method's success, medical experts said the treatment, which is based on the method used by breeders of exotic and endangered animals, may be replaced by a technique called "vibratory stimulation," which is cheaper and can be performed at home.

Mammaries Are Made of This

Mark Carriere, owner of an adult video firm in Chatsworth, California, filed suit against a special effects company because the fake breasts he ordered for an actress to wear in a movie didn't look realistic enough. Carriere ordered size 99Z.

Potatoes may be used for breast implants, according to researchers at a Dutch potato processing company in Avebe. They received a government grant to see if starch made from potatoes can replace silicon in implants.

U.S. Tax Court judge Joan Seitz Pate ruled that exotic dancer Cynthia S. Hess, known professionally as "Chesty Love," was entitled to claim a $2,088 deduction for depreciation on the surgical implants that enlarged her bust to 56FF. The Internal Revenue Service had rejected the deduction, explaining that expenses to enhance a taxpayer's appearance, while useful for business, are too personal to be a business expense. The judge ruled that the implants increased Hess's income and that she couldn't derive personal benefit from her breasts because "they were so large that they ruined her personal appearance, her health, and imposed severe stress on her personal and family relationships."

School officials in Pinellas County, Florida, suspended teacher Patricia Locke after she pleaded no contest to drunk-driving charges but reinstated her when she argued that she wasn't intoxicated, just disoriented because her breast implants had ruptured. Dr. Frank Vasey, a University of South Florida physician, helped Locke persuade a school board hearing that the confusion and memory loss that led to her arrest after she drove erratically and hit two other cars were typical symptoms of women suffering from silicon poisoning.

During an argument outside the Mons Venus Club in Tampa, Florida, a 75-year-old man shot nude dancer Dora Oberling, 30. Paramedics said that her silicone breast implants "might have saved her life" by deflecting the bullet aimed at her chest.

After she was involved in a traffic accident, Donna Vallah of Nashville, Tennessee, thought at first she had suffered no injuries, then reported that within a month after the accident her left breast implant started to deflate. By the time she had surgery a month later, the right implant had also deflated. Vallah sued the other driver. The jury awarded her $11,500 to cover the cost of replacing both implants, despite a deposition by plastic surgeon Dr. Ronald Gilmer that the right breast deflation was not caused by the accident. He stated implants have been known to "deflate for no reason."

The third issue of *Oneworld* magazine showed Asian model Zhing topless, while a similar photo of the model

Julianne appeared with black bars over her breasts. The magazine explained the decision was made by *Oneworld*'s printer, who said Zhing's breasts weren't big enough to be offensive.

Aud Sto of Flekkefjord, Norway, sued the general interest picture magazine *Se og Hoer* for 150,000 kroner—about $22,000—for publishing a photograph of her walking topless along a Canary Islands beach. She charged that the photo caused people in her straitlaced town to taunt her, and said the picture was hurting her bakery business.

After newspapers reported the lawsuit story, Inger Marie Maylam of Kristiansand came forward and insisted that she was the woman pictured, adding that she wasn't the least bit offended. "The breasts are mine and they are for free," she told the *Dagbladet* newspaper. "It's wrong for somebody else to try to make 150,000 kroner on them."

Neither woman could remember being photographed, but *Se og Hoer* editor Knut Haavik commented, "I take it for granted that people are able to recognize their own breasts."

Steve Marek, a hypnotist in Frankfort, Kentucky, announced that he could help women enlarge their breasts as much as one full cup size using hypnosis. He claimed that during puberty some women suppress the growth of their breasts for one reason or another. By enrolling in his 12-week course for $375, Marek said, women can unlock their potential.

After a newspaper in Fort Worth, Texas, reported police were seeking a woman with a rose tattoo on her left breast as a robbery suspect, at least 300 people called to say they knew such a woman.

Archaeologists digging in the shallow water of Germany's Lake Constance uncovered four pairs of 6,000-year-old human breasts fashioned from clay. The life-size clay breasts, dotted with white paint, were apparently once attached to the wall of a building, making them the oldest wall decoration ever discovered in central Europe.

Convinced that her breast implants were causing her immune system to go awry, Laura Thorpe, 39, of Bloomfield, Arizona, used a blade from a disposable razor to cut open her left breast and remove the silicon gel herself. Thorpe said her insurance company refused to pay for the operation because the implants were listed as cosmetic and doctors told her the operation would cost $5,000, which she didn't have. Instead, she learned how to perform the operation by visiting a doctor at the Veterans Administration hospital in Albuquerque, who described the procedure for her. "I just listened and went home and did it myself," she said, explaining that she waited until her husband and three children had gone to bed, then made the incision by following previous incision lines. "My thinking was that 100 percent I'm going to die and if I do it I have a fifty-fifty chance of maybe living," she said, "and I'll take that over dying."

Japanese actress Etsuko Nami, 45, filed a lawsuit against the chief surgeon at a Tokyo hospital because he botched the plastic surgery on her nipples, causing her scheduled nude photo book to be canceled. Nami said the operation left her with no left nipple and only part of the right one.

Bernie Carson filed a $200,000 personal injury lawsuit against P.T.'s Show Club, claiming Busty Heart, a performer at the Belleville, Illinois, strip club, caused him "emotional distress, mental anguish, and indignity" when she slammed her large breasts into his neck and head. Carson also insisted he was "bruised, confused, lacerated, and made sore" by Heart's 88-inch chest. Her breasts reportedly weigh 40 pounds each.

Paul Shimkonis, 38, filed a suit in Pinellas County, Florida, seeking $15,000 in damages from the Diamond Dolls nightclub, claiming that he suffered whiplash when a topless dancer hit him with her oversize breasts, which he described as being "like two cement blocks." To avoid a long and costly court battle, Shimkonis chose to take his case before *The People's Court* television show. After court officer Josephine Longobardi examined the dancer's breasts, then reported that they weighed about two pounds each and were 20 percent silicone and the rest natural, arbitrator Ed Koch, a former mayor of New York, ruled against Shimkonis. According to the show's producer Harvey Levin, Koch conceded that the breasts may have hit Shimkonis, "but he is not convinced they caused any injury."

A woman went to a hospital emergency room in Frisco, Colorado, complaining that her breasts were making a "swishing sound." An X ray revealed that the cause was trapped air in the woman's saline implants. According to Dr. James Bachman, who treated her, the air expanded in the Rocky Mountain town's high altitude.

Police in Sheffield Lake, Ohio, charged Michael Copp, 18, with stealing his mother's credit card to pay for his girlfriend's breast implants. "For this type of misuse, this is the first we've ever seen," Sergeant Tony Campo said. "And we've seen everything."

Timex awarded $15,000 to Peter Doughty, a British civil servant who invented a machine that precisely measures women's busts. According to *The Guardian* newspaper, Doughty got the idea from his brother, who suggested using a box with light-emitting diodes and sensors to measure children's feet, not just length and width, but also height. Doughty's wife asked if the device might measure bosoms, since she had read that seven out of ten women had ill-fitting bras. Doughty patented the design and said he would use the Timex "innovation award" to perfect his working prototype.

LipoMatrix Inc. introduced a new breast implant filled with salad oil. "It's natural, safe, and secure," said company president Terry Knapp, who predicted the $250 million worldwide market for breast implants "is going to increase substantially," especially in Asia.

The Food and Drug Administration tentatively endorsed a way for women to grow their own breast implants. Researchers at Carolinas Medical Center and the University of Michigan explained that the procedure involves removing a suitable tissue sample from a woman's thigh or abdomen, using it to grow additional cells in the lab, then implanting the cells in the woman's breast with a biodegradable breast-shaped scaffold. The scaffold is metabolized within weeks, and the cells should multiply and mature into real breast tissue, according to scientists working on the project, who said they believe the cells will fill the space left for them by the scaffolding and then somehow know when to stop growing.

Publisher Norm Zadeh announced that his new magazine, *Perfect 10*, would depict only nude women who have not had breast implants. "I've been to strip joints and fallen in love. And then you realize they're not real," Zadeh said, adding that he wants readers to know "what real breasts look like, because they've forgotten."

The New York Transit Authority announced that women may ride subways topless. Officials qualified the new policy by saying that bare-breasted women must not violate any transit rules, such as smoking or chewing gum, or create a "disruptive or dangerous situation in the subways." Agency spokesperson Jared Lebow foresaw little problem, explaining, "New Yorkers, especially subway riders, are exceedingly blasé."

In a divorce case in Hendersonville, Tennessee, Carol Ann Bennett asked Circuit Judge Thomas Goodall to award her custody of her breast implants. Noting that her estranged husband, Warren Woodrow Bennett Jr., had the implants, she explained that she had had them removed after contracting lupus but left them behind when she moved out of their condominium. She told the judge that she wanted them for a lawsuit against their manufacturer but feared Warren would destroy them. "Divorce granted to wife," Goodall ruled, "breasts to be returned to wife."

Taylor Monet, 33, an exotic dancer at Boston's Soiree club, claimed to have the world's first inflatable breasts. A valve-and-hose implantation allows her to inject or extract a saline solution to vary the size of her silicone breasts between a minimum 40-inch bust and a maximum 96-inch measurement.

Love and Marriage

Carmen Friedewald-Hill, 26, shot boyfriend Ryan Gesner to death in Frederick, Maryland, during an argument over which one of them loved the other more.

A conference of Italian bishops issued an edict, warning that remarried divorcees, unmarried couples, and separated Roman Catholics could receive church sacraments only by promising to give up sex.

Shopkeeper Khalid Mosood, 27, wrote more than 700 letters proposing marriage to his girlfriend in Galle, Sri Lanka. She turned him down and married the letter carrier.

Jeff Flentge and Deena Petot were exchanging wedding vows in Perryville, Missouri, when a former classmate, Sherry Ann Korando, 25, rose from her seat in the middle of the church and fired two shots at them, then rushed outside and killed herself with a shot to the head. Police said that although Korando knew the couple only slightly, they found a yearbook photo of the groom in her wallet.

Vicki Long filed a lawsuit in Atlanta demanding child support from the Reverend Donal Keohane, a Roman Catholic priest whom she accused of fathering her daughter. When blood tests proved conclusively that Keohane couldn't be the father, Long contended that Keohane should be ordered to pay anyway. Keohane conceded that he once agreed to provide $350 a month to support the child but only as a desperate compromise to keep Long from publicizing her charge.

A 32-year-old Sacramento woman announced she was suing a local hospital for $100,000 because for 20 years she couldn't perform oral sex as well as she should have been able to. The woman accused the hospital of leaving a piece of tubing in her throat after an operation in 1978. She coughed it up three days later but now insists that as a result of the incident, she has a "feeling" that something is caught in her throat and "is not able to give her partner the joy and pleasure that she thinks is his due."

Fourteen death row inmates in California filed a lawsuit in U.S. District Court asking the state to allow them to father children through conjugal visits or artificial insemination. One of the inmates named in the suit, Herbert J. Coddington, was sentenced to death for killing his two children in a custody dispute with his wife.

According to the inmates' attorney, Carter R. King, the suit contends that laws banning prisoners from procreating constitute cruel and unusual punishment. Acknowledging that the Supreme Court has denied past requests for conjugal visits for condemned inmates, citing security, King noted, "Obviously, artificial insemination doesn't create a security risk."

Salt Lake City police said a 43-year-old woman reported that a man she knew broke into her house, ordered her to undress, pulled a pillowcase over her head, bound her hands and feet, took her picture, then forced her to drive to Elko, Nevada, and marry him.

A woman in Salt Lake City dialed the 911 emergency line after her husband refused to have sex with her. According to the police report, the husband rejected her advances because he was watching a basketball playoff game between the Utah Jazz and Los Angeles Clippers. The enraged 27-year-old wife swung at her husband, who deflected the blows while keeping an eye on the close game. The Jazz won, and the woman was taken to the hospital with arm injuries.

Broward County, Florida, Circuit Judge Paul Marko offered some advice to a woman whose divorce case he was hearing. "You've got to go out and get another guy," he told Marianne Price, 33. "The singles bars are full of them. I've been there, I'm a single man. There are all kinds of bimbos in those places, and there are all kinds of guys running around in open shirts with eagles on their chest. There are great guys out there. . . . You'll find them in singles bars, there are wacky brain surgeons out there. You go—you go find a brain surgeon."

Marko also forbade Price from having a male live in her house, although he said her ex-husband, Gordon Price, could have anything he wanted in his home, including the "entire Dolphins cheerleading squad running through his apartment naked."

Some 4,000 would-be bridegrooms in India set off for a traditional "marriage bazaar" in Saurath in northern Bihar state in search of end-of-the-season bargains from the guardians of women who previously failed to attract a husband. Only 10 to 15 prospective grooms found a match, however. Village elders said the others hurt their chances with inflated dowry demands.

During divorce proceedings, Xu Cheng-shun, an actor with a Beijing opera troupe in Shanghai, attacked his wife in the courtroom and bit off her nose. He explained that his action was a desperate attempt to save his marriage, reasoning that if she was disfigured nobody else would marry her.

Three single men from a farming village in northern Japan spent five days in 1990 driving a tractor 434 miles to Tokyo, where they paraded around the city hoping to lure prospective brides for them and 74 other single men in their district. The men, feeling no one would marry them because they were farmers, started the stunt two years earlier as a way to impress urban women. Media coverage of the first tractor parade drew about a hundred women and led to four marriages. The next year, 53 farmers from 11 districts took part in a procession of 20 tractors. Again there were four marriages. By the third year, despite waving banners reading MARRY ME AND COME TO MY PLACE, the three farmers were unable to interest any city women.

Marjorie Proops, Britain's equivalent of Dear Abby, who for nearly 40 years advised readers on how to keep their marriages together, disclosed that she carried on an affair with a lawyer for 30 years of her 53-year marriage. "He taught me so much about sex," she said.

Ben Freedman, managing director of London's Prince Charles Theatre, announced the cinema was installing love seats, complete with condoms, for romantic couples in the back row. "Fifty percent of people who go to the cinema are out on a date," he explained, "so I decided to make it easier for them."

Authorities in Pemberton Township, New Jersey, accused Forrest D. Fuller, 28, of murdering his girlfriend, then taking her corpse to West Virginia with the intention of marrying it. Just after crossing the Pennsylvania-West Virginia state line, Fuller reportedly stopped at a tavern and tried to strike up a conversation with the barmaid by telling her that his dead girlfriend was outside in the car. After he showed her and a man working at the bar the body of Jodie Myers, 20, in the backseat, sheriff's deputies arrested him. They also found a wedding dress in Fuller's trunk.

Town councilors in Hearst, Ontario, voted to end the tradition of locking prospective bridegrooms in cages in the center of town. While on public display, the men usually have eggs and tomatoes thrown at them by townspeople, who pay for the privilege in part to raise a nest egg for the couple, although in one recent incident a would-be groom was given an enema with a grease gun. The councilors acted after local clergy pointed out that some men were so fearful of the practice that they were forgoing marriage altogether.

Railroad officials in the German state of Schleswig-Holstein offered half-price fares to couples who kiss at the ticket window. "With this ticket, we want to say to all young people that riding the train should not just be comfortable but fun, too," said railway business manager Goetz Dietsche, adding that participating couples must wear special identification stickers for their journey and be prepared to kiss on demand for conductors.

Twenty Muslim men attending a weekend prayer service each returned home with a new bride and money for a honeymoon. The *East African Standard* newspaper reported that when the cleric at a mosque in Garissa, Kenya, announced to the congregation that the women were available, "more than 40 men trooped to the front of the mosque to take a glimpse of the girls." Deciding that it was improper for the men to choose their brides individually, the cleric ordered the women to put on veils, then married 20 couples and gave each bridegroom $335.

Charles Washington, 21, was found shot to death in Houston after a weekend quarrel with his gay lover. Police said the fight started when Washington discovered that his lover had been having an affair with his mother, who lived in the house with them.

When One Isn't Enough

Donald Flood, 40, was sentenced to prison in Arlington, Virginia, for bigamy after he married three women within 45 days. He blamed his wedding spree on drugs. When he realized he had three wives, Flood said, "I didn't care. I wanted to love someone."

Dallas lawyer Brian Loncar was charged with bigamy after a ceremony at a Las Vegas wedding chapel while he was still married to his first wife. Loncar explained that he didn't think he was breaking the law because the marriage was performed by an Elvis Presley look-alike. "He said they got married by some guy that looked like Elvis Presley, that it was a phony deal," assistant District Attorney Norman Kinne said. "Well, not necessarily. Not in Las Vegas."

A 58-year-old double amputee in Winnipeg, who was charged with bigamy, received a year's probation after telling a Manitoba court that his lesbian wife had threatened to leave him unless he married her lover. "Geraldine said that if I married Mary-Lou, she would be a wife for me and a husband for her," Albert Ducharme said. His lawyer, Randy Minuk, called it "the most bizarre, weird case I've ever had—and I've had some weird ones."

Five years after Pan Oi-lin was convicted of bigamy, the Hong Kong High Court annulled her original 14-year-old marriage to Leung Cheung. The court overturned the conviction, ruling that Pan had not followed the traditional Chinese wedding ceremony because she had failed to present her in-laws with a cup of tea.

Police in Woonsocket, Rhode Island, investigating the death of Tammy Petrin, 21, accused her husband Ronald Harnois, 41, of bigamy. They explained that while courting Petrin two years earlier, Harnois called himself Roland and claimed it was his twin brother, Ronald, who was married to Joanne Harnois. Petrin didn't find out the truth until she and Harnois had been married for two months. After that, the three became close friends, often bowling together, although Joanne Harnois didn't discover the nature of Ronald's relationship with Tammy until police charged him with trying to kill Joanne by attaching six pipe bombs to her car. Tommy Petrin had agreed to testify against him in the bombing case just before her murder.

Having too many wives proved embarrassing to Sir Wiwa Korowi, the new governor-general of Papua New Guinea. When he chose Nancy, the younger of his two wives, to accompany him to London when he was going to be sworn in by Queen Elizabeth, his senior wife, Sonya, complained about being snubbed and accused the country's "Big Man" of making himself small by not acknowledging all his wives and children when taking office. She demanded a divorce, but while negotiations for a settlement were under way, a former wife previously unknown to the public, Ellepe Nomi, who divorced Sir Wiwa in 1985, entered the fray, seeking revenge against Sonya. "We were happily married until she came in," Nomi charged. "She is not his first wife. If she didn't stick her nose into our marriage, we would not have separated."

William Huston, 59, escaped prosecution for bigamy, despite living with both women in the same apartment. According to a complaint filed by Maria Huston, 28, she met William Huston in the Philippines, where she lived. They married and moved to an apartment in Chaska, Minnesota, near Minneapolis. She told police that her husband left the area to find work and returned a month later with a woman named Linda, who was also from the Philippines. He told Maria that he and Linda were divorced but that she was sick with cancer and needed someone to care for her. He said he was giving Linda the downstairs portion of their apartment, and told Maria to stay upstairs and Linda to stay downstairs. When he left the apartment, the two women talked to each other, and Maria discovered that Linda was not sick and was still married to Huston. She waited six months to file her complaint, and the police took two years to catch up with Huston.

Melissa L'Anore Bullock, 21, pleaded guilty in McComb, Mississippi, to bigamy, admitting that she married Truman Fourroux, then married Michael Shelby Lowe two days later. Her attorney, Bruce Thompson, explained that she only went through with the second marriage because she didn't think the first one was legal.

"Which one of these husbands do you want to keep?" Circuit Court Judge Joe N. Pigott asked her.

"Neither one," Bullock replied. "I'm too young to be married."

Accused of having two husbands at once, Cathy Garoutte Campbell DiNickle, 33, told prosecutors in Erie, Pennsylvania, that she did not remember already being married to Art Campbell when she married Paul DiNickle the year before.

Martinsville, Virginia, preacher Elwood Gallimore, 44, announced that he had taken a 16-year-old bride to join him and his 42-year-old wife of 26 years. Authorities admitted they couldn't charge him with bigamy because his second marriage was a religious rite performed without a license, although they did charge him with two counts of seduction and taking indecent liberties with a minor. Gallimore explained that he was only obeying God's will because polygamy is in the Bible. "I'm standing on God's word," he declared, "regardless of what the law does."

Kuwait's Charity Committee for the Marriage Project urged married men to take more wives (up to the Islamic legal limit of four) in order to deal with the problem of "spinsterhood." Saying there were too many unmarried Kuwaiti women, the charity offered men as much as $2,800 in loans, cheap kitchenware, and free furniture.

In Thailand's Chantaburi province, when Pratuang Bamrungchiep, 28, announced he was marrying Thabthim Kachabal, 18, her younger sister threatened to commit suicide if he did not also marry her. Although bigamy is illegal in Thailand, Pratuang agreed to marry Aurathai Kachabal, 16. More than 500 well-wishers attended the wedding.

Vernon Pierce, 33, surrendered to authorities in Glendale, Arizona, after a three-month marrying spree netted him four wives in two states. He said he told them that his job required him to travel, but that was a lie. "I didn't have a job," he explained. "I didn't have time." Besides having four wives, Pierce was dating other women. Police who searched his home found a list of women's names on a 3-by-5 card headed "Who to Marry."

Kenneth Dunn lived two lives for 18 years in identical homes with matching kitchens and wallpaper, his widow Pat, 54, told a court in Birmingham, England. The other woman, Jean Cooper, 56, waged a bitter legal battle against Pat Dunn over the right to be buried beside him, ultimately winning, a judge said, because she had paid for the double plot.

Kinky Is As Kinky Does

Police in Palmerston North, New Zealand, arrested Shane Patrick Neho, 17, and a younger accomplice for breaking into Barbarella's sex shop. The suspects fled with a blow-up woman, a female mannequin dressed in rubber underwear, a large drinking mug shaped like a vagina, and an inflatable sheep. "We have not yet ascertained why a sex shop should be stocking blow-up sheep," Sergeant Ollie Outrim told the *New Zealand Herald*, "especially as Palmerston North has a large sheep population."

After a woman reported that a heavy, sweating man crawled up behind her on his hands and knees and sniffed her buttocks at the library of California Polytechnic State University in San Luis Obispo, investigator Ray Berrett staked out the library and observed a 40-year-old nonstudent sniff the behinds of at least seven women.

Flemington, New Jersey, Superior Court Judge Edmund Bernhard sentenced Federico Fernandez, 47, to 10 years in prison for squirting soap on women shoppers, offering to clean up the spill, then fondling them as he wiped it off. Fernandez's lawyer, John Furlong, said that the attacks were a cry for help.

Police and paramedics in Lakeland, Florida, rescued a 33-year-old man trapped in a motel swimming pool. They reported that "his pants were down to his knees and his penis was stuck in a suction hole." Paramedics inserted a lubricant around the suction fitting, and after about 40 minutes were able to free him.

David Joseph Zaba, 32, pleaded guilty in Denver to assault for pouring varnish on his wife during sex instead of the honey and chocolate syrup she was expecting. Angela Zaba said that the varnish made her hair fall out. The police report on the incident said the couple had been using food as part of their sex life for six or seven years, noting that the wife "stated that this is not the first time that he has used varnish, but she has had enough, so she called police."

A 40-year-old man, who was arrested in Florida's Dade County after propositioning an undercover policewoman posing as a prostitute, mounted a defense based on the fact that he did not ask the woman for sex but rather if he could spank her. "The act of requesting a spanking is not prima facie evidence of sexual activity," argued the man's public defender. Explained the accused, "I had seen a study on corporal punishment on the news and wanted to try it out, so I asked to spank her bottom."

Police in Madison, Wisconsin, reported that a man dressed only in a diaper and a garter belt chased two women down a city street begging them to spank him.

The Boston area was plagued in 1992 with several incidents of children receiving Barbie dolls for Christmas and opening the gifts to find pornographic photos in the boxes with the dolls. The photos featured both men and women in various sexual positions and inscriptions on the back of each describing Barbie engaged in such activity.

A 60-year-old San Clemente, California, grandmother, arrested in a prostitution investigation, reportedly ran a "sex dungeon" in which a naked man choked to death on the end of a dog leash. "We were just playing," said the grandmother. A coroner's officer noted, "Nobody forced him to be tied up and shackled in black leather."

Police in Peterborough, Canada, arrested a 26-year-old man discovered in a women's public outhouse by a woman using the facility. The woman happened to peer down through the toilet seat and saw him looking up at her. Police theorized that the man climbed down through the seat into the outhouse holding area.

Harry Veltman III, acting as his own lawyer against charges that he sent Olympic gold medal figure skater Katerina Witt some 60 threatening letters and nude photos of himself, asked that his jury be made up only of nymphomaniacs and atheists. Santa Ana, California, Judge Gary Taylor said no.

Police in Colorado Springs, Colorado, accused Donald James Brown, 59, a retired grocer, of clipping people's pictures from the newspaper and superimposing their heads on photos from pornographic magazines. They said he sent the pictures to at least 39 of the people with threats to kidnap them and make them perform oral sex acts.

Police in Cook, Australia, accused Thomas Borkman, 24, of breaking into the apartment of a 31-year-old woman who had never met him and super-gluing his face to the sole of her foot while she slept. Emergency surgeons needed three hours to separate his face from her foot. A police official speculated that Borkman's motive "had some sexual significance."

Police in Clayton, Missouri, charged dog food salesman Roy McCarthy, 36, with dropping gallon jugs of wine on the toes of three grocery store workers, then posing as a doctor and trying to rub their feet. Tipped off by store officials who grew suspicious when injury reports kept coming in for wine bottle–related injuries, police said McCarthy would start talking with a store employee, then drop the bottle during the conversation.

At least 55 women reported being attacked in Midtown Manhattan by a man who blew darts at their backsides before police arrested Jerome Wright, 33. Charged with blowing darts at women in skirts in New York City, Wright claimed he was innocent, insisting that the real Dartman could be from an island where women "who wear provocative and inappropriate clothing" are tossed into volcanoes. Wright did not name the island.

Police in Nashville, Tennessee, arrested David W. Osbourne for mooning women at shopping malls, saying the 23-year-old suspect, who wears women's dresses and no underwear, may have been responsible for more than 20 cases of exposing himself to shoppers. "He just follows them out to their cars, and when he arrives at the car he moons them and has an object in his rear," said Officer James Buford Tune, who noted police refer to the suspect as "The Carrot Man."

Fumes from a cigarette betrayed a Peeping Tom in Colmar, France. The smoke drifted into the next-door bedroom through the hole he had bored in the wall, alerting the occupants.

Police in Toledo, Ohio, reported they were investigating at least five break-ins they believe to be related because of the intruder's bizarre behavior. In one incident, he smoked a cigarette after defecating in a cat litter box and urinating near the kitchen stove while the homeowner slept on a nearby couch. Another time, a 30-year-old woman who found her dresser drawers in disarray said one of her undergarments had been dropped in the middle of the kitchen floor. She added someone apparently slept in her bed after placing plastic bowls from the kitchen at the end of the bed. Police Sergeant Robert Baumgartner said that although small amounts of cash were taken in some of the incidents, apparently money wasn't what the intruder was looking for, noting, "He's excited by this, but why? I guess we'll have to ask him that when he's arrested."

Yoichiro Iino, the mayor of Kitakata, Japan, offered to reprimand himself and cut his salary in half for six months to atone for peeping into a women's bath. The incident occurred during an official inspection of the newly opened city-run spa, when the 72-year-old mayor walked into the women's dressing room and peeped through a glass door where about 20 naked women were bathing. The mayor insisted he was just checking attendance at the new facility, explaining, "I was worried about how turnout would be after the free-entry promotion ended."

In 1994 Duluth, Minnesota, was plagued by the "diaper bandit," a man who broke into homes to steal diapers and women's underwear and then left the items, soiled, outside the homes—on lawns, inside newspaper delivery boxes, hanging from fences, and on the shrubbery. Some of the victims received obscene phone calls from a man saying, "I'm wearing your diapers. Would you change my diapers?"

Police in Brookfield, Michigan, arrested a 20-year-old man after he was found banging on the door of the "Perfect Sitters" child care center dressed in an adult-size sleeper, holding a teddy bear and diaper bag, with a pacifier in his mouth.

A 31-year-old man in Anchorage, Alaska, was labeled "Dr. Diaper" by police, who said he would answer ads from women offering child-care services and tell them that he was hiring them at rates of from $12 to $20 per hour to take care of "Tommy," an adult who was the mental equivalent of an 18-month-old child. After saying he would send "Tommy" over, the "doctor" would then show up himself, dressed in a diaper. He would often defecate in the diapers in front of the women, sometimes masturbate, and never pay the bills.

A 25-year-old man from Holladay, Utah, was charged with perversion and trespassing in a series of incidents in the Salt Lake City area. He allegedly showed up at day care centers wearing baby clothes and diapers and convinced the day care center operators to let him into their facilities under the pretense of various stories, including that he was a fraternity pledge or was being punished for cheating on a university exam. The man wore a pink dress, bonnet, and diaper and had a pacifier in his mouth. While in the center he often had his hand inside the diaper, telling people that his diaper was too tight. He also ate baby food and sucked on a bottle. Investigators linked the man to a series of such strange incidents going back at least seven years.

A St. Louis police officer was accused of stopping at least 10 female drivers on the pretense of giving them a minor traffic ticket. The women said he would tell them to sit in the backseat of his cruiser, then remove their shoes, explaining that shoes were a potential hiding place for drugs. Next he would place their feet on the front seat and either fondle, tickle, or merely look at them.

A 53-year-old male nurse in Oregon was charged with pandering obscenity after police found that he had photographs of male corpses developed at a photo developing store. Employees of the store contacted police after viewing the photos, which showed some of the corpses posed in various positions on metal tables. According to the sheriff's department, the man had been fired by one hospital for "spending too much time with cadavers." Police noted that almost all the bodies featured gunshot or stab wounds along with autopsy incisions. The man later told investigators that he was a homosexual and found the photos sexually exciting.

Police in Red Bluff, California, charged a man with abducting and then imprisoning a 20-year-old woman in his home as a sex slave for seven years. The woman was kept in handcuffs and restraints in a box in the man's basement for a year before being moved to a larger crate. Neighbors were at a loss to explain the situation, noting that the woman in recent years had held several jobs, including working as a hotel maid. One neighbor called the pair "as normal as anyone."

A man in Tifton, Georgia, was convicted of public indecency after a series of incidents in which he threw chunks of lard at women while driving around in the nude. Police, who had dubbed him the "Crisco Kid," apprehended him after a car chase when he was seen driving through a shopping center parking lot slinging lard at his favorite targets.

An unidentified man in his twenties driving a maroon sports car entered a York, Pennsylvania, convenience store at 5:25 one morning and picked up a can of whipped cream. The man, dressed in a T-shirt and a disposable diaper, approached the counter with the can.

"What are you going to do with that?" the clerk asked.

The man responded, "The diaper or the whipped cream?"

"Both," the clerk said.

The man then shook the can and sprayed whipped cream into a hose sticking out of his diaper. He left the store and drove off in his sports car. Police said that the incident was the third of its kind that they could remember.

A 27-year-old Milwaukee man was arrested 40 times for dressing in women's clothes and spying on women in public rest rooms. His fortieth arrest came after a woman complained that he had looked under her rest room stall. The man explained to police that he was just visiting the rest room to read a porn magazine, dropped it on the floor, bent down to pick it up, and just happened to glance under the neighboring stall. A court-ordered psychological report noted, "It appears that with considerable frequency the defendant's days may be virtually filled by pursuing these activities."

Boulder, Colorado, police apprehended a 36-year-old man after a car chase begun when the suspect attempted to run over a shopping mall security guard. The guard had approached his car after reports that the man had been sitting in his vehicle for more than an hour in the mall parking lot completely naked except for a covering of shaving cream reaching from his shoulders to his groin. He also wore clear plastic wrap around his stomach.

St. Louis police said they ended the city's "Birdman" attacks when they arrested a 28-year-old man. They accused him of grabbing three women in a public park, fondling them, then running off while flapping his arms like a bird. According to Detective Sergeant Leo Forsting, the suspect "admitted doing this to some 12 women over the last six months."

Police in Crown Point, Indiana, responded to the home of a 76-year-old woman who said she awoke from sleep to find a strange man tickling her feet. A suspect was arrested nearby. The 50-year-old man admitted breaking into the house, saying that he was "looking for water."

During a two-day period at least four women studying in the campus library at Brigham Young University had their clothes cut while they slept in their study carrels. In each case, the woman awoke to find an unknown man sitting next to her who was not there when she fell asleep. None of the women noticed the damage to their clothing until after they left the library. "This individual is using a knife,

razor-knife, razor blade, or some similar cutting instrument to cut away clothing, primarily from the armpit and
hip area of his victims," campus police said. "None of the
victims have been cut themselves, only their clothing." A
fifth victim had about three inches of her ponytail cut off
in the library while she studied, again not noticing it until
later in the day.

Little Things Mean a Lot

Police in Peabody, Massachusetts, charged Gilbert DaSilva, 46, with slicing another man's penis during an argument over the comparative sizes of their organs in a downtown bar. Police Captain J. Stephen Begley said that the dispute climaxed when the victim "exposed himself" and DaSilva pulled a knife and slashed at the victim's organ, almost severing it. The victim, said to be in his fifties, went to the hospital, where his penis was surgically reattached.

A man in his mid-thirties, whose penis was cut off by a lawn mower blade while he was trying to repair the mower, was rushed to Froedtert Memorial Lutheran Hospital in Wauwatosa, Wisconsin. To prevent the tissue from dying before the organ could be reattached a week later, surgeons attached the organ to the man's arm.

Californian Jim Boyd announced the formation of a group called Hung Jury to promote the idea that men's penis size really does matter to women.

Boston psychiatrist Albert Gaw identified a condition called "koro," which strikes mostly Chinese and

Southeast Asian men, causing the victims to believe their genitals are shrinking. Koro epidemics in China have caused victims to use strings, clamps, and even tight-gripped friends to keep their organs from disappearing.

Miami surgeon Ricardo Samitier told *Cosmopolitan* magazine that he can add both length and thickness to men's penises by suctioning fat from the lower abdomen and injecting it into the organ. He declared that his procedure "dramatically improves self-esteem."

Within weeks of opening the government's first sex shop, Adam and Eve, China's government reported it was unable to stock enough penis enlargers to meet the demand. Wen Jing-feng, who manages the shop, said that 85 percent of the 200 to 300 customers a day were men. He noted that another best-seller was a spray claiming to keep the penis erect and prevent AIDS at the same time.

Police in Cologne, Germany, arrested a man on suspicion of killing his blind, 74-year-old father during an argument by cutting off his penis with a knife or scissors, then leaving him to bleed to death. Chief investigator Klaus Lidert said police couldn't find the penis, and the suspect claimed he was too drunk to remember what happened.

Justin Williams, 25, filed a $1-million malpractice suit against the doctor who directed his sex-change operation at the University of Virginia Hospital. He said he was told he would receive "the Cadillac of penises" but claims his prosthetic penis failed to match what was promised. Williams explained that he "has never been able to urinate through his 'penis,' much less have sexual intercourse."

Cynthia Mason Gillett, 28, of Waynesville, North Carolina, was accused of pouring nail polish remover on her husband's penis and setting him on fire while he slept. Although Gursham Gillett, 27, refused to testify against his wife, she admitted responsibility and received two years' probation.

Authorities in Anchorage, Alaska, accused Sarah Louise Achayok, 36, of biting through the skin of her boyfriend's penis after learning he was cheating on her. Officers answering an emergency call reported finding the injured man sitting on a couch with blood on his face, shirt, and the crotch area of his long underwear. They said he told them, "his old lady bit him."

According to court documents, a medical exam showed "a serious circumferential bite to penis that completely penetrated the full thickness of the foreskin." Swelling prevented surgeons from sewing up the damage.

While Clifford A. Roby, 34, was serving time in Keene, New Hampshire, for kidnapping a New Hampshire woman and making her drive to Vermont, he cut off his penis with a Bic disposable razor and flushed it down the toilet. He declared it was God's will that he be punished.

Terry Grice, 26, drove 60 miles to a Dothan, Alabama, hospital with his severed penis and testicles in the back of his pickup truck. He told police that two men had jumped him and cut off his genitals with a circular saw, which investigators found at the scene of the incident. Three weeks later, Grice admitted that he had cut off his organs himself, using a crude wooden device he made himself to hold them in place while he sliced them off with the saw. He explained that he was "depressed."

A Chinese homemaker used scissors to snip off her sleeping husband's penis, hoping to improve her love life. The *Heilongjiang Legal News* reported that the woman was following the advice of a soothsayer, who said "if she wanted her marriage to be as good as it was at the beginning, she should wait until her husband is drunk and then use scissors to cut off his penis so he can grow a new one."

Jesus Sandoval filed a $1-million lawsuit against Contra Costa County, California, and its hospital in Martinez for amputating his penis when he sought treatment for a painful sore. His suit contends that a circumcision and antibiotics would have been sufficient.

Earl Zea, 34, reported that he was sleeping when a burglar entered his home in Johnstown, New York, and cut off his genitals with a pair of sharp pruning shears, after which he drove himself to the hospital and underwent emergency surgery. A week later, the victim admitted that he had clipped his own penis, explaining he was trying to discourage a man who was attracted to him. County District Attorney Polly Hoye said Zea would be charged only with falsely reporting an incident, noting, "It's not against the law to remove your own penis."

In Turkey, Mehmet Esirgen, 52, tried to cure his sexual impotence by having a penis transplant—using a donkey as the donor. The wire service Agence France-Presse reported that three times Esirgen brought home a donkey, amputated its sexual organs, and appealed in vain for a doctor to perform the operation. Apparently the third time so annoyed his family that his son shot him in the leg. Esirgen announced that as soon as he recovered from the shooting, he intended to buy a fourth donkey.

When the stock market crashes, so does the male sexual organ, according to Dr. Alexander Oshanyesky, an Israeli specialist on blood vessel problems. He said a drug used by his clinic to treat a test group of 193 men for impotence failed to do the job when Iraqi Scud missiles slammed into Israel in the 1991 Gulf War, and when the Tel Aviv Stock Exchange crashed in 1993. "The stress causes the adrenaline level to shoot up, moving more blood to the brain and the heart and less to the penis— total impotence," Oshanyesky said, adding it could take time for markets and men to rise again. "When a man is sexually impotent he loses confidence and has trouble making financial decisions."

Mass circumcision ceremonies could be turned into a tourist attraction in Malaysia, according to Culture, Arts, and Tourism Minister Sabbaruddin Chik. "By charging tourists a small fee to watch such cultural events, the organizational costs can be covered," Chik told *The Star* newspaper after attending a ceremony in which 48 boys were circumcised, adding tourists would "enjoy watching something that was different from the norm."

Alan Hall, 48, ran into a woman he knew as Brenda at a gas station in Fairfield, California, and invited her back to his brother's house, where they had sex. Afterward the woman reportedly made a statement implying she wanted revenge for Hall's conviction years earlier for murdering a friend of hers. Hall told police the woman then cut off his penis and fled. It was found eight hours later on his front lawn, but by then it was too late to reattach the organ.

After a 38-year-old woman was abducted and groped by a man in a pickup truck when she hitched a ride in Prince William County, Virginia, she forced her abductor to release her by grabbing his genitals, then picking up a whiskey bottle and threatening him with it. "She did not release his genitals," police Lieutenant Barry Barnard said, "until he stopped and unlocked the door and she got out."

Ronald Elmore turned up at the Bossier Medical Center emergency room in Bossier City, Louisiana, with both his testicles cut off. He told police that an unknown woman he picked up in a bar castrated him while he was sleeping. Later he changed his story, saying that he and his wife had been taking drugs, and when he was unable to perform sexually, he told her to castrate him. Finally Elmore admitted he had castrated himself and put his testicles in a freezer, where police found them.

Joe Solino Jimero was publicly beheaded in Saudi Arabia for stabbing and beating surgeon Rashid Abu Jabal to death after the doctor reattached his penis. Authorities said Jimero had cut off his penis himself because he wanted to become a woman.

Six California men filed lawsuits against a Culver City doctor billing himself as the world's leading authority on "penile augmentation" surgery. The suits contended that the procedure done by Dr. Melvyn Rosenstein to make the men's sexual organs bigger instead left them numb, infected, and deformed.

Similar complaints from men in Los Angeles and San Francisco who responded to ads for a growing number of doctors offering penis-enlargement operations prompted a team of urologists from the University of California at San Francisco to investigate whether the procedure is necessary or cosmetic. After measuring 60 volunteer urology patients, the researchers concluded that a "normal" penis during an erection would be anything greater than 2.8 inches long and 3.5 inches in circumference. From these measurements, they reported that only about 2 percent of all men might actually need the surgery to lengthen and thicken the organ. One of the researchers, Dr. Tom Lue, said the procedure, which costs up to $6,000 and has proved dangerous and disfiguring, is "basically done so men can show off in the locker room."

In Germany, Heidemarie Siebke, 50, was charged with slicing off her former lover's penis with a bread knife after he badgered her for sex. Prosecutor Anette Bargenda said that after the accused mutilated Hans-Joachim Kampioni, Siebke then set his apartment on fire to cover up the crime.

Brazil's government canceled a $5-million safe-sex campaign featuring a talking penis after two groups complained. The Catholic church objected because the television ads promote condom use, which Raimundo Damasceno Assis of the National Council of Brazilian Bishops said encourages sexual promiscuity. People with the name Braulio protested because that was the chatty organ's moniker. Braulio is a common family and first name, but Health Minister Adib Jatene cited a survey showing it also is a common nickname for a penis. First to threaten a lawsuit was São Paulo law professor Braulio Monte Jr. He insisted that having a talking penis named Braulio on TV could damage him professionally.

A man arrived at a Wichita, Kansas, hospital emergency room with his erect penis stuck through a seven-and-a-half-pound barbell weight. The gentleman explained to emergency workers that he wondered if his penis would fit through the hole in the weight. Once it was in and erect, he could not withdraw it. After twelve hours, during which the fire department failed to cut the weight, a urologist was summoned to drain blood from the penis and free him.

Domingo Morales, 67, who was hospitalized in New York City after his penis was severed, told police an enraged prostitute did it. Two days later, he admitted making up the story to avoid ridicule, explaining that he really cut himself while making a guitar, which he had propped between his legs. The organ, which Morales had saved in a Tupperware container, couldn't be reattached.

Angry mobs in Ghana lynched or beat to death at least 12 "sorcerers" who took part in a scheme where the sorcerers touch men, then tell the victims their penises will shrink or disappear unless they pay for an antidote. Inspector General of Police Peter Nanfuri ordered increased police patrols and vowed to call in the army to maintain order. Meanwhile, newspapers reported that medical experts tried to calm the panic by going on television to "explain in detail why penises increase and decrease in size," but such assurances have been of little help, even in Ghana's capital, Accra, where Deputy Police Commissioner Kwashievie Agbelie told state television that police examined all alleged victims and found their genitals intact.

Elsewhere, seven men were beaten and burned to death in Ivory Coast's commercial capital of Abidjan by angry mobs accusing them of being penis shrinkers. Local police dismissed the threats of penis shrinking as a ploy by thieves to cause a crowd to form so they could rob people. Police commanders ordered all impromptu gatherings dispersed in an effort to prevent the attacks from spreading.

A 54-year-old truck driver in Gallatin, Tennessee, filed a $10-million lawsuit over a defective penile implant, which he said "took all the manhood from me." His attorney explained, "He could be just walking down the street, and it would erect on its own."

A registered sex offender in San Francisco was admitted to a psychiatric ward after construction workers found him trying to cut off his penis with a broken bottle. The naked man, identified as 50-year-old Robert Schlumbohm, had almost succeeded when he was found at a downtown construction site, said Officer Jim Taylor.

In Bridgeport, Connecticut, police called to the scene of a shooting found Kevin Hall, 18, lying on the ground clutching his groin. His pants, which had a large hole, were still smoking. He explained he was the victim of a drive-by shooting, but his girlfriend said Hall had bragged about having a sawed-off shotgun in his pants. When he tried to pull it out to show it to her, it fired, blasting his genitals. To add to his woes, police charged Hall with possession of the weapon.

The Dutch penis isn't getting any bigger, according to psychologist Erick Janssen, disputing claims to the contrary by the Netherlands Association for Sexual Reform. That research body, which advises the government on standards and sizes for condoms and also sells them, reported it had noticed a growing demand for larger sizes. Pointing out that Dutch men and women are getting bigger all the time because of improved diet and health care, the association concluded that penises must be getting bigger, too. Janssen, who was hired by an Amsterdam condom shop whose owner wanted to know whether it should be stocking a wider range of condom sizes, said the only way to answer the question was through clinical measurements. His research determined that the average circumference when erect is 4.84 inches—the same as a 1948 study found.

Army surgeons in Beijing announced they successfully crafted a new penis for six-year-old Jiang Rongming, using his own skin and abdominal tissue. Xinhua news agency reported that Jiang's original penis was bitten off by a donkey he was petting outside his home.

A 47-year-old man who broke down the door of his ex-girlfriend's apartment in Beloit, Wisconsin, found her with a 58-year-old man. According to police, the new boyfriend shot the ex-boyfriend once in the penis. When the gun jammed, the old boyfriend attacked and bit off a three-inch chunk of the new one's ear.

When Raquel Nair Lucio, 33, of Tiete, Brazil, learned that her husband Luis Carlos Ferraz, 61, had impregnated another woman, she cut off his penis with a kitchen knife. Lucio told São Paulo state police that she was inspired by news reports of three similar attacks in Brazil in the past month.

In the first of those cases, a jealous Brazilian cut off the penis of a man he thought to be the lover of his ex-wife in the southeastern state of Minas Gerais.

In the other instances, an evangelist wife cut off her husband's penis because she was fed up with his weekend smoking and drinking, and a jealous girlfriend severed her cheating boyfriend's penis during a spat.

An article in the *Journal of the American Medical Association* warned people against attempting to increase sexual pleasure by rubbing cocaine on their genitals or injecting it into their urethras. The focal point of their article was the case of one 34-year-old man who occasionally injected cocaine into his penis. The last time he did it, he experienced a painful erection lasting three days. Twelve days after the incident, he had developed gangrene in his penis, and it fell off while bathing.

A Clearwater, Florida, woman put public prosecutors in a quandary after she said that the man who burglarized her home and attempted to rape her had a very distinguishing mark on his penis. She said that she was sure that the man's urinary opening was not in the usual spot at the front of the penis but rather was on top of it. When informed of the victim's claims, the incarcerated suspect agreed to have photos taken of his erect penis. When shown to the victim, she noted that his urinary opening was in the standard place and said that it could not have been her attacker.

China's *Guangxi Daily* reported that a father of three was fined 3,000 yuan (about $350) by the government after his wife gave birth to a son in violation of the state's one-child policy, which seeks to control the country's population. Joking in front of his two daughters, aged six and seven, the father looked at his son and said, "A 3,000-yuan fine for this little penis! We should just cut it off." Later, while the father worked in the fields, his daughters cut the baby's penis off and the infant bled to death. Upon learning what had happened, the father beat the girls to death and committed suicide.

During the 1980s and 1990s China's most celebrated surgeon was Dr. Long Daochou, who specialized in work on penises, specifically penis extensions and replacements for men who somehow lost their originals. Known for his ability to create new penises that had real sensitivity, the doctor's exploits became legend and his successes were widely reported in the press, which routinely listed the lengths of his new creations. "The beauty is that they have sensitivity," Long said. "Nobody in the world does it quite like this. I give men a brand-new life."

Long explained that he assembled his creations from skin flaps, muscle and nerve fragments, bone shards, and sponge tissue taken from other parts of the patient's body and also some material scavenged from cadavers.

The San Jose, California, fire department was called in to free a 30-year-old man who managed to lock a large padlock around his genitals. According to the fire captain, "He was pretty uncomfortable. We used our bolt cutters and sliced through the metal." As to how the lock got there in the first place, the captain said, "I didn't ask."

Frenchman Henri Cousteau, 33, of Marseilles inherited a 9¾-inch penis after his best friend, Paul Simone, was killed in a car crash and his will left the organ to Cousteau for transplant. "I never had real sex," Cousteau said. "Paul had hundreds of women. Now I could have the same success."

A jealous Thai wife in Nakorn Ratchasima cut off her husband's penis, tied it to a helium-filled balloon, and let it fly off, police quoted the victim as saying. Prayoon Eklang, 47, was rushed to the hospital when he discovered his angry wife's handiwork. "I woke up and ran looking for it but a neighbor said my wife had already tied it to a balloon and let it fly away," he told police. Prayoon said he believed that he was drugged by his wife and fell into a deep sleep minutes after he had dinner and woke up to find blood gushing from the lower part of his body.

At least a hundred men in Thailand were revealed to have undergone bogus penis-enlargement operations, the *Bangkok Post* newspaper reported, noting that the so-called doctors who performed the surgery injected the men's penises with a mixture of olive oil, chalk, and various substances to provide bulk. One official at a hospital in Chiang Mai told the paper, "I've even seen penises containing bits of the Bangkok telephone directory."

The Honeymoon Is Over

After a Saudi woman donated an eye to restore her husband's sight, the man left her for another woman. According to the newspaper *Al-Jazirah*, the man explained he couldn't stand the sight of his one-eyed wife.

Marital bliss turned into a family feud at a wedding in a Los Angeles suburb. Police said the early morning brawl began when two 12-year-olds, one a relative of the bride and the other a relative of the groom, got into a fight, and the adults argued over who had started the fight. "When I got here, all of them were going at it. Nearly all 150 of them," said Sergeant Jim Ferris of the Monrovia Police Department, who added that 10 of the guests were injured and five were arrested.

After spending four years fighting Florida prison officials to marry a death-row inmate, Wanda Eads, 51, finally was wed to Frank Valdes, 33. Four months later, he took her name off his visiting list. The next month, Valdes sued for divorce, claiming the marriage was "irretrievably broken." "This is insane," Eads said, insisting she still loves him and that the only legitimate grounds to dissolve the marriage is adultery. "Why does a death-row inmate need a divorce?"

Police in Middleton, Ohio, arrested ex-spouses Clarence Wilkinson, 44, and Melissa Frances, 43, for hiring the same hit man to kill each other. The alleged hit man, Christopher Brown, 19, reportedly told police that Wilkinson contacted him and offered him a gun and $12,500 to kill Frances. She said Brown told her about the deal and posed the possibility of killing her ex-husband for $15,500. Frances said she gave Brown a $500 down payment and a knife, which she later retrieved in an attempt to call off the deal, whereupon Brown tried to extort money from her not to kill Wilkinson.

After four months of marriage, Margaret Anne Hunter, 24, of Alexandria, Virginia, discovered that Thorne Wesley Jameson Groves, 26, was not the man for her. In fact, Groves, whom Hunter had met through an America Online "chat room," was really Holly Anne Groves. Before they met face-to-face, Hunter said, Thorne Groves told her he had AIDS and proposed a quick wedding because he had only a short time to live. Explaining he was concerned about transmitting AIDS, he restricted intimacy to petting and fondling over his clothes and even wore a prosthetic penis to further the deception, according to Hunter.

After becoming suspicious, Hunter eventually confronted Groves, who admitted deceiving her but gave no explanation. Besides seeking an annulment, Hunter filed a $575,000 fraud suit against her husband to recover, among other things, the cost of the lavish wedding her parents paid for.

A judge in Kenosha County, Wisconsin, sentenced Kimberly Borrego, 32, to a month in jail for ramming her husband, Manuel, with their car. The incident occurred on the couple's wedding night after they got into a fight over how loud to play the radio.

In Romania, Florica Ifrimie hanged herself before her wedding after she and her fiancé could not agree on the menu for their wedding banquet.

A bride-to-be on the Greek island on Crete suffered a nervous breakdown the night before her wedding when she took friends to the couple's new home to see her gown and discovered the groom in the arms of his best man. "What was really upsetting for her was that he was wearing her wedding dress when she caught him in their own bed," a police officer in Heraklion told the Athens news agency. "Her family has sworn revenge if they ever find him."

After a year of marriage, Marius and Roxana Dumitrescu filed for divorce in southern Romania, citing "irreconcil-able differences." According to court records, Marius wanted Roxana to wear mauve clothing, as his mother always did, but she preferred dressing in white, red, and green.

Police in Port Jervis, New York, charged Luis Deleg, 27, with fatally stabbing his new bride, Tina Entwistle-Deleg,

30, at a party hours after their wedding. The two began arguing when Deleg accused his wife of being interested in his cousin, according to Lisa Quinones, the bride's sister and maid of honor, who said, "I heard love, honor. I didn't hear kill in any of that ceremony."

Veneline and Mariete Vassilevi divorced after being married only a week when they learned they are twins. Agence France-Presse reported that the 25-year-olds were raised in an orphanage before being adopted by different families, one in southern Bulgaria, the other in Varna on the Black Sea. They met as students at the Varna Institute of Economic Science but learned their true relationship only after Veneline brought his bride to meet his natural mother, who fainted on seeing her daughter.

Japan's first divorce magazine chose the name *Liz*, after Elizabeth Taylor. "When Japanese think of the people associated with divorce," Chizuru Taguchi, the editor in chief, explained, "the Hollywood actress Elizabeth Taylor often comes to mind."

On the morning of her wedding, a 36-year-old San Bernardino County, California, probation officer had to bail her fiancé, Frank Cisco Bridges, 43, out of jail on burglary charges. She went through with the ceremony, but the groom was arrested and charged with raping a seven-year-old girl at the reception after luring her to an upstairs bedroom with the promise of a dollar. Police said that Bridges, who has AIDS, told them he wanted sex and had propositioned two women at the party, only to be turned down.

When newlyweds Laurette Kenny, 38, and Raymond Brunson, 50, got into a fight at their wedding reception, police said she threw macaroni salad at him, and he responded by shooting her in the stomach.

One-legged, wheelchair-bound Mabel Hyams, 79, was found guilty in London of beating her husband, Harold, to death with a plastic bedpan. Prosecutor Anthony Wilcken explained that she killed Harold Hyams because he had affairs with three women early in their marriage and taunted her about them for the next 40 years.

John Alvin Jackson of Trenton, South Carolina, admitted giving his estranged wife to another man to settle a $200 debt because he was "red-hot mad" at her. After getting her to go with him under the pretense of spending a long weekend together trying to reconcile their marriage, he suggested they stop by Frank William Yeck's place in Grovetown, Georgia, to pick up a Bible. There, Jackson handed her over to Yeck, who placed her in bondage and forced her to participate in various sexual activities before she escaped the next day.

At Yeck's trial, he testified the woman was a willing participant. "I showed her how to enjoy sex," he said. "Pain was the objective to a certain extent." Jackson, who testified against Yeck as part of his plea bargain, said Yeck had assured him he would not harm her. Afterward, Jackson said Yeck told him, "It's nothing serious. The marks will go away in a couple of days. I know what I'm doing."

Objects of Affection

After *The Deseret News* ran a story about three Salt Lake City women receiving large envelopes that contained their bras and panties, 11 more women called police to report receiving similar packages. One said she got five of her items along with $12 and a note telling her the money was to cover other underwear the thief wanted to keep. The women didn't know they had been burglarized until they received the packages in the mail. The police also heard from a man who received a package containing $10 and a note from the thief explaining he couldn't find any women's underwear in the house, so he stole a *Playboy* magazine.

Thai police arrested Buddhist monk Samai Parnthong, 35, after catching him having sex with the corpse of a 40-year-old woman in a temple during the third night of her funeral. Unable to find a law against necrophilia, they could charge him only with damaging the coffin.

Police in Spokane, Washington, arrested Wendell Ray Bryant, 35, after finding 100 women's high-heeled shoes in his home. Bryant had been arrested several years earlier in connection with 162 high-heeled shoes found at his home—and another 500 in a self-storage unit he rented.

A judge in Ventura, California, granted the request of a paroled panty thief that the court return to him 300 panties, bras, and bodysuits that he had stolen before his arrest but that remained unclaimed by his 12 victims. However, the judge ruled that the man, who was a landlord, could not have his two-way mirror back and returned that to his parole officer. In the past, while not busy stealing underwear, the thief had installed the mirror in his house in order to covertly videotape his female tenants bathing.

A 63-year-old retired trash collector was arrested by police on suspicion of criminal mischief after a number of stores in the Denver area reported that scores of women's bras had been slashed. In each instance only the right cup of each bra was cut. After leaving a Woolworth's where he had purchased a pair of panties the suspect was arrested when the clerk who waited on him discovered eight damaged bras. "There's some psychological significance [to the slashing of the right cup], I'm sure," said a police spokesperson.

Four women reported that a man looking like Kenny Rogers fondled their hair while they were watching the movie *Sleepless in Seattle* at a theater in Grosse Pointe Woods, Michigan. The incidents occurred over an eight-week period, according to Detective Steve Backlund, who said that at least two of the victims believe the man may have been sucking on their hair "because the girls actually found the end of their hair was wet."

An immigration agent at Toronto's Pearson International Airport was suspended after he ordered people entering Canada to remove their shoes and socks. The agent, who officials acknowledged had been counseled four times for similar complaints, told visitors that official policy required them to remove their footwear so he could photograph their feet.

Ross Watt, 28, was arrested in Edinburgh after he was found just before eight o'clock one morning on a city sidewalk with his pants pulled down having sex with a shoe. "If you have to do things like this," Sheriff Richard Scott admonished him, "then you can do them in private."

Prehistoric artifacts generally identified as tools were actually sex toys, according to British archaeologist Timothy Taylor. Objects carved as phalluses, widely found in Upper Paleolithic art, have been prudishly interpreted as spear straighteners or batons, Taylor said, pointing out these so-called batons "fall within the size range of dildos." He suggested they have been mistakenly identified as ritual objects because of "a modern belief that premodern sex was essentially a reproductive activity, and that if it wasn't, it ought to have been."

After Amtrak personnel in Springfield, Massachusetts, reported a "ticking sound" coming from a suitcase in the storage area that a passenger had checked through in advance, police evacuated the building. According to Lieutenant Robert Thibodeau, officers then opened the

bag and discovered the noise was coming from a vibrating sex toy.

Tokyo police charged Yoichi Ishihara, 29, with breaking
into 150 school locker rooms a total of 300 times after
they found 1,200 pairs of schoolgirls' panties in his apartment. He explained that he started stealing the underwear
as a hobby but then became aware of the value of schoolgirls' used panties for sale to fetishists. Underwear is such
a dominant theme of Japanese pornography that there are
even vending machines that dispense schoolgirls' used
panties.

A 51-year-old man notified police in Long Branch, New
Jersey, that someone had stabbed him in the crotch while
he slept, cutting off a half inch of his penis. Investigators
quickly determined, however, that the real culprit was a
vacuum cleaner and that the man had tried to find sexual
gratification from the appliance's suction. "But what he
didn't realize is that there's a blade in the vacuum cleaner
right under where the hose attaches that pushes the dust
into the collection bag," Long Branch Public Safety
Director Louis Napoletano said, explaining that when the
man turned on the vacuum cleaner, the blade cut off part
of his penis.

Chuck Jones, former publicist for Marla Maples, admitted having a sexual relationship with her shoes that went
beyond a fetish after investigators found nearly 50 pairs
of Maples's shoes, boots, and sneakers, as well as her
panties and bras, at his Midtown New York office. "Things

were pulled out of places you couldn't imagine," Detective William Lynch testified at a hearing on evidence. "Shoes, underwear, boots from behind file cabinets, from behind radiator covers. It was the most amazing thing I had ever seen." After a judge ordered a retrial of his 1994 conviction, Jones told jurors that Maples "knew about my secret interest in shoes and shamelessly played up to it."

Britain's Family Planning Association, which receives $3.3 million a year from the government to dispense advice on sex and contraception, announced it would begin selling vibrators and other sex aids by mail order. A spokesperson explained the move was prompted by "people wanting this kind of confidential service"— particularly the disabled and house-bound who had no other way of getting such aids.

The family planning body insisted that its intention was not to titillate or encourage sexual experimentation. "We want to de-stigmatize sex aids for people," the spokesperson said. "We would be very much at the boring end of the market. We're not talking about blow-up dolls or handcuffs."

A former concrete traffic barrier dumped in a San Francisco park years ago started being worshipped as a religious shrine by pilgrims arriving from as far away as India. Hindus and New Agers alike pray, meditate, and make offerings to the phallic fetish. According to park gardeners, a city worker dumped the 4-foot-tall carved stone traffic barrier in Golden Gate Park, where it lay unnoticed until local Hindus saw it and decided it was a symbol of devotion to the deity Shiva. As worshippers flocked to it, devotees asked parks officials for permission to build a permanent shrine over it, raising the issue of separation of church and state and prompting city parks director Mary Burns to seek the rock's removal. Worshippers said they would go to court to keep the rock where it is.

Khalid al-Mathkour, chairman of the higher consultative committee for the preparation of the implementation of Islamic law in Kuwait, issued a *fatwa*, or religious advisory, calling for a ban on the Barbie doll. "The curves of the body are too similar to those of an adult woman," he explained.

Gender Benders

Bruce Jensen, 39, of Bountiful, Utah, discovered that his wife "Leasa" of three and a half years was a man. The deception by Felix Urioste, 34, unraveled when Jensen filed a missing-persons report and learned that Las Vegas, Nevada, authorities had arrested Urioste for using fraudulent credit cards, which had been issued to Bruce and Leasa Jensen, to run up at least $40,000 in debt. Urioste was traveling as a bearded man.

Authorities said the feminine-looking Urioste, who already had his testicles, but not his penis, removed in anticipation of a sex-change operation when he met Jensen at the University of Utah Health Services Center while masquerading as a female doctor, never let Jensen see him naked during their celibate marriage. Jensen wed Urioste out of a sense of obligation after Urioste claimed to be pregnant with twins after their lone sexual encounter. Urioste later said the twins were stillborn. "I feel pretty stupid," Jensen said, adding that he wanted an annulment, citing irreconcilable differences.

A transsexual living as a woman made a national list of most-wanted deadbeat dads. The National Council of State Child Support Enforcement Administrators reported that William Henry Reid, who had a sex-change operation in 1985 and is now Billie Jean Reid, 43, owes $53,000 in child-support payments.

A woman judged to have Italy's most beautiful legs was disqualified from competing in the Miss Italy pageant after officials discovered that she was born a man. Giovanna Fanelli, 27, born Gianni Fanelli, had both male and female sex organs until undergoing an operation a year before the pageant to remove the male organ.

The winner of a nationwide Oprah Winfrey look-alike contest run by *Ladies' Home Journal* magazine turned out to be a man. Jacquin Stitt, a city water department worker, denied misrepresenting himself as a woman, explaining that he was undergoing a sex change.

Italian businessman Paolo Edoardo Boeris, 27, married Riam Kuemjan, 33, of Thailand, whom Boeris believed to be a woman but who turned out to be a man. At the hearing before the Thai court that eventually annulled the marriage, Boeris's attorney explained that the couple had sex several times, always in the dark.

Prosecutors in Colorado Springs, Colorado, charged Sharon Lee Clark, also known as Sean O'Neil, with sexual assault and criminal impersonation after the 19-year-old woman spent more than a year masquerading as a man and allegedly having sexual intercourse with at least three teenage girlfriends. One girl said that she had sex 15 times with Clark, while another claimed 12 times. The third said that she had sex with Clark "51 times this year, every other day from May to September."

Police in Muskegon, Michigan, charged Mari Louise Medacco, 17, with having tricked two high school girls into thinking she was a boy and having sex with her on several occasions. Calling herself Mario, Medacco wrapped her chest in bandages, feigning rib injuries, had sex only in the dark, and wore an artificial penis.

Portuguese authorities arrested Tito Anibal da Paixao Gomes after neighbors complained that he failed to repay money they had lent him on the promise of being repaid by his military pension. A check of military records found that Gomes wasn't the retired army general he claimed to be. What's more, a physical exam revealed that he wasn't even a man. The police said Teresinha Gomes had fooled her neighbors for 18 years, adding that the phony general's wife had learned the truth after five years of marriage when she wandered into the bathroom one day and discovered Gomes's true gender.

After two weeks in the women's cellblock of Norway's Stavanger District Jail, a 30-year-old Peruvian prisoner arrested with a false passport notified prison guards that "she" was really a man. According to Oslo's *Verdens Gang* newspaper, the prisoner, who was arrested wearing heavy makeup and women's clothing, was assigned to the women's cellblock after a body search at the airport and a strip search at the jail. "It seems pretty clear," Police

Inspector Leif Ole Topnes said, "that our body-search techniques aren't good enough."

When a female prostitute in Charleston, West Virginia, quoted two men a price for oral sex, a man in drag offered to undercut her price. The men turned out to be under-cover police officers, who arrested elementary school principal George Meadows, 55. After police photographed him in a wig and lipstick, Meadows pleaded guilty to solic-itation.

A Sri Lankan who won a government award after being selected as the country's 1995 female entrepreneur of the year was arrested—for being a man. Police said Sattambige Sriyaratne, 36, impersonated a woman for about three years, received bank loans amounting to $500,000, and ran a successful business exporting prawns. "He had posed as a wealthy woman, well con-nected to some leading government personalities," said police inspector Mohamed Nizam. "That and his forced female charm are probably what made him a successful businesswoman." The female impersonator was also legally married to a 29-year-old man.

A Saudi religious court sentenced a man to 200 lashes and six months in prison for wearing a dress to a wedding party in the city of Hael. The man reportedly dressed as a woman to get a surreptitious look at women he might want to marry.

A Spanish judge approved a request by two convicted transvestites to wear women's clothes while serving sentences at a men's prison in Villabona. Judge Marisa Llaneza said the two were entitled to wear feminine clothing, just so long as it was "decent." One of the transvestites, convicted robber Maria Jesus Lastra, 27, had charged wardens with discrimination for confiscating all his dresses and constantly harassing him and a transvestite cell mate for having breasts.

A custody battle in Santa Ana, California, took an unusual turn when the mother of a three-year-old girl claimed the girl's father is actually a woman. Kristie Vecchione, 27, said her husband became a man through sex-change operations more than 20 years ago. Vecchione was impregnated by artificial insemination.

Brazilian transsexuals are entitled to free sex changes under new rules that classify the operations as experimental. Explaining that transsexuals were carriers of a "permanent psychological distortion in their sexual identity," officials at the Federal Council of Medicine said the only conditions for patients who want to have their penises removed were that they be older than 21 and undergo two years of hormone treatment and psychological counseling. Newspapers reported that gleeful transsexuals immediately began lining up for operations, which usually cost $15,000. "I've been dreaming about this for so long that I'd already given up hope," one São Paulo nurse told the *Folha de São Paulo* newspaper.

More people are changing sex and going to Thailand to do it, according to a seminar in Bangkok on sex-change operations. Reuters news agency reported that the lure is the quality and natural look of Thai-made sex organs. The surgery costs about $5,000 for a man to become a woman and $10,000 for a woman to become a man. "Thailand has become the most popular place for sex-change operations," seminar organizer Dr. Nikorn Dusitsil of the Institute of Medical Science Research said. "Many foreigners are coming here to have the surgery, and I think the income from this area will be able to help shore up the economy to a certain extent."

Eddie James Mundell, wanted by the FBI after being declared absent without leave from the Marine Corps in 1968, turned up nearly 30 years later as Erica Sandra Kay, who was wanted on fraud charges stemming from having four husbands at the same time. "She suckered all of us," said Ammadell Whitsell, whose nephew John Bowers, 50, married Kay in 1996 while she was still married to two other men. After running off with his new Mercury Mountaineer, a gold watch, and $90,000 in cash, the following year Kay married her fourth husband, Ralph Caruso, 68. "She convinced him she was a successful interior designer," said FBI agent Tim Coakley, who noted that Kay had a sex-change operation two years after deserting the Marines. "They set up shop in St. Petersburg, and she started running up bills. She told him she was pregnant. They even went so far as to put a nursery in the house." Coakley said the FBI was mere days away from catching up to Kay, when she drove off with Caruso's Cadillac.

After compiling a professional record of 20 wins and two losses, Thai kick boxer Pirinya Kaibusaba, 16, finally made his debut at Bangkok's Lumpini Stadium. His biggest challenge wasn't his opponent but the weigh-in before the bout. Pirinya, a transvestite who powders his nose during training, wore makeup and pink nail polish to the weigh-in but broke into tears when he learned that fighters at Lumpini Stadium must be weighed in the nude in front of officials and reporters. Softened by his sobs, Lumpini officials eventually let him step on the scales in his underwear. *USA Today* reported the 140-pounder then went on to pummel his opponent.

Canada's armed forces agreed to pay for sex-change operations after one of its soldiers requested such an operation and a military assessment concluded that changing gender would not restrict the performance of military duties. Colonel Scott Cameron, director of medical services for the military, said that the cost of such operations, including hormone treatments and psychiatric counseling, would be between $30,600 and $61,200 in U.S. currency. "There are some things that these patients sometimes have done cosmetically, like breast implants and so on," Cameron said. "We would not pay for that."

Attorneys representing convicted murderer Damon Alejandro Christopher Bowie in Prince George's County, Maryland, Circuit Court, tried to show that his upbringing made him psychologically unstable. Key testimony was presented by his transsexual parent. L.A.—formerly Linda

Anne—Bowie said that his son used to call him "Ma," but when he was about 10 years old started calling him "Pa."

Some New York legislators expressed fear that a state law might encourage indigent transsexuals to commit crimes in order to receive free estrogen treatments. The law provides hormones for prisoners who received them before their conviction. Representative Michael Nozzolio noted that the state spends $700,000 a year on estrogen for 87 male prisoners who are becoming female.

London subway officials announced a plan to end confusion among ticket collectors by issuing riders who are undergoing a sex change two identity cards. One will be for the rider as a woman, the other as a man.

City officials in Willowick, Ohio, demoted the fire department's first female captain to the entry-level rank of firefighter. They cited Megan Parsons's job performance, insisting that her demotion after 20 years with the department as Captain Garry Strater had nothing to do with her sex change.

Lake County, Ohio, Probate Judge Fred V. Skok issued a marriage license to two people who announced they were lesbians, even though one of them was a man. Paul Smith, who dresses in women's clothing and applied to have his name changed to Denise, said he expected to complete his sex change within three years. Because Ohio law specifies marriage is a partnership between a man and a woman, Skok withheld the license until he got a doctor's note certifying that Smith still has male sex organs.

Minnesota's Medicaid program has funded sex-change operations for as many as 10 persons since 1987 and has approved such surgery for several others who have been unable to find a physician to perform it, according to Chris Reisdorf, policy coverage supervisor in Minnesota's Department of Human Services. Noting no other state Medicaid program funds sex-change surgeries, *The Washington Times* reported the state's Medicaid program covers the operations when they are deemed to be "medically necessary"—that is, to aid transsexuals who say they are "trapped" in the bodies of the opposite sex and whose lives may be so disrupted by their perception that doctors prescribe surgery.

Women commuters in Tehran beat up an Iranian man who rode on a bus dressed as a woman to win a $33 bet with his father. The newspaper *Ettelaat* reported that the 31-year-old man, identified only as Mohsen, rode in the segregated female rear section of the bus, but his large body and shoes gave him away. After the women beat him up, a court sentenced him to 20 lashes for committing "an ugly and improper" act.

The 1995 gold medal winners in men's volleyball at Thailand's national games did not get to represent their country in international competition because the 12 men wore women's clothing. The teammates had plastic surgery, grew breasts, and wore heavy makeup, but had not yet "changed our sexual organs" to become women, according to team coordinator Patphong Srinutham. Compared with most societies, Thais generally are more tolerant of cross-dressers, and some were surprised when told that fans from other countries might jeer if cross-dressers played in an international match. To avoid conflict, the winners bowed to the inevitable. "We have to admit that we want to be beautiful, wear makeup, long hair," team player Pitsanu Pleankum, 32, said. "So we know and accept that we cannot be in the national team and have to think about our country's reputation."

Dennis Smith, 36, an inmate at Florida's Martin Correctional Institution, filed a lawsuit against the state because he was denied estrogen, which he said he needs to "match his physical appearance with his inner feelings." Smith, who goes by the name Rhonda, said that he had sex-change surgery, including breast implants, but needed hormone treatments to remain a woman.

Atlanta police charged Fred Kennedy Glenn with the death of a transsexual, who died while getting an illegal silicone injection to make his rear end fuller. Dallas Denny, director of the Atlanta-based American Educational Gender Information Service, noted that Atlanta has developed a reputation as a center for back-alley silicone shots among transsexuals who cannot afford sex-change operations. She explained, "People look at it as a quick and easy way to feminize themselves."

A 27-year-old Taiwanese woman who had a sex-change operation to become a man faced being called up for military service. An official in Chungho City, who noted that under Taiwan law all men who graduate from high school and are under 28 must serve two years in the army, said that the person, identified only as a Mr. Chen, "like other men, is no exception and cannot be exempted from military service."

Darryl Malone, 29, filed a complaint with the Nevada Equal Employment Opportunity Commission after he was fired, charging his employer with sexual discrimination for repeatedly passing him over for promotion because he was a man. For eight months, the 165-pound ex-Marine impersonated a woman on a phone-sex line for Northwest Nevada Telco.

Can't Help Myself

Doctors at Bulgaria's Kozloduy nuclear plant found that workers were being exposed to above-average levels of radiation. They also concluded that the higher radiation boosted the workers' sex drive. Kozloduy psychiatrist Galina Palieva noted that increased potency had been observed among workers exposed to radiation, and that wife swapping at the sprawling complex was rife.

A 48-year-old man in Hennepin County, Minnesota, was accused of using his status as a Mason to coerce a woman into having sex. The woman said the man stopped by to drop off some information on the Masons for her husband, who was seeking membership in the Masonic Temple. After grabbing her, handcuffing her hands above her head, and beating her with a leather strap, he told her that if she didn't cooperate with his sexual advances her husband would not become a Mason. The victim said she was afraid to report the incident for fear of jeopardizing her husband's chances.

Two prisoners admitted having sex while awaiting arraignment in a Berks County, Pennsylvania, courtroom less than 10 feet from Judge Stephen B. Lieberman. The 21-year-old male and 23-year-old female were in a 6-by-12-

foot holding cell with two inmates, whose accounts of the episode to other prisoners led authorities to reprimand the couple. "They are not allowed to do what they did under our rules," Warden George A. Wagner said.

Pennsylvania State Senator Dan Delp, 33, a conservative Republican elected on a "family values" theme, announced he would not seek reelection after a state grand jury charged him with having sex with a 19-year-old prostitute, buying the underage hooker liquor, then seeking reimbursement from taxpayers for his date, which he claimed was a business dinner to discuss "banking issues."

A 30-year-old crew member aboard a Greek luxury yacht touring the Aegean Sea became angry when a passenger rejected his amorous advances, so he grabbed a hatchet and attacked the captain, who had reprimanded him for his overtures, and another crew member. He then tried to set fire to the private yacht, but the seven Canadian and four Greek tourists aboard managed to extinguish the blaze. Finally, the sailor doused himself with gasoline and set himself on fire.

A 38-year-old man from Wheatfield, New York, was hospitalized after attempting to castrate himself with clamps, a scalpel, and a local anesthetic. He told Niagara County sheriff's deputies that he had to do something to lower his sex drive.

When police in St. Petersburg, Florida, charged Wayne David Sorg, 29, with exposing himself in public, the suspect offered the explanation that he used to be a male stripper and missed the attention he got onstage.

Virgin Atlantic Airways canceled a massage service on Tokyo flights after Japanese businessmen assumed they were getting more than a gentle rubdown. "It became clear that in Japan the implications of offering a massage are distinctly different," said Virgin chairman Richard Branson. He explained that Virgin's masseuses had to become adept at politely correcting the misunderstanding "to the evident disappointment of some of our passengers."

After a New York state office worker complained that his desk smelled like it was being used for sex, supervisors set up video cameras and recorded two state maintenance workers having sex numerous times on the desk. The two were dismissed.

The Reverend Roy A. Yanke, 37, pastor of Covenant Alliance Church in Beverly Hills, Michigan, pleaded guilty to robbing 14 banks for $47,000. Investigators said Yanke told them he spent the money on prostitutes to satisfy his "tremendous appetite for sex."

James Scott, 24, of Fowler, Illinois, was sentenced to life in prison for sabotaging a levee on the Mississippi River during a 1993 flood. Prosecutors said Scott told friends that he moved some sandbags to flood an area so that his wife could not return from her job on the Missouri side, because he wanted to have affairs and party.

Judy Pruitt, 23, of Houston had six children by six different men, but Children's Protective Services took four of them from her. When a *Houston Post* reporter asked her why she continued having children, she explained, "I have to keep replacing the ones they take."

In Wels, Austria, Roman Catholic priest Peter Nenning, 32, astonished 500 parishioners during Sunday services by telling them he was quitting the priesthood because he could no longer endure celibacy. "It's no good," he announced from the pulpit. "I can't go on."

A U.S. Postal Service letter carrier in Syracuse, New York, complained to police that for four months a woman on his route had chased him into the street and begged him to have sex with her. He said the woman also exposed herself when he delivered mail to her house.

During the first seven months of U.S. peacekeeping efforts in Bosnia, at least 70 soldiers were shipped back to Germany because they were pregnant. The newspaper *Stars and Stripes* reported favorite spots for fraternizing were bunkers, latrines, and backseats of Humvees.

San Diego police charged Tammy Jo Garcia, 27, with 25 counts of arson in two years, explaining that fires stimulate her sexually. Two men, identified as Garcia's lovers, were also charged, one of whom admitted starting fires to impress Garcia so she would have sex with him.

A Tampa, Florida, court sentenced a 27-year-old woman to five days in jail for telephoning her local police department just to say "I love you." She called on the emergency line at least 19 times during one eight-hour shift and up to eight times in a single hour.

Eight inmates broke out of their cells at the Nashville, Tennessee, city jail. While trying to escape, they found themselves in the women's cellblock. They postponed their escape plans to engage in sex with female inmates and were still at it when guards tracked them down and apprehended them.

You've Come a Long Way, Baby

The Toronto City Council voted to replace the word *manhole* with the nonsexist term *maintenance hole*, despite objections from Councilwoman Maureen Prinsloo. "Women are sensible enough," she pointed out, "that they don't go down these stupid things."

The federal Bureau of Prisons took a step toward equal treatment of inmates by issuing a new rule banning women prisoners from wearing wigs. Previously only men had been denied the privilege.

Iranian Deputy Education Minister Hossein Herati assured critics of new classes on family planning for female high school students that they would not actually discuss sex. Instead, he said, the classes would deal only with the problems caused by the population increase.

Germany's liberal, mostly male Free Democrats launched an equal rights campaign to open the army to women, attacking the legal exclusion of women in combat as the country's last sexist job ban. Their female counterparts rejected the call to arms, however, charging the men with raising the equal rights banner only because the number of men entering the armed forces had fallen.

Malaysia's Islamic government banned female public servants from wearing lipstick and announced that only unattractive women would be hired for public service jobs, so that men won't be distracted from their work.

After complaints increased that women passengers were being molested by men pressed close to them on packed subway trains in Seoul, the Korean National Railroad announced it was designating two cars on each 10-car train as women-only. When the service began, men passengers continued crowding into the women's cars. Subway officials conceded that they are powerless to enforce the rule but did say they would continue the policy in case the men decided to comply.

A municipal official in Tehran announced that seating and standing room on the city's minibuses would be separated by gender. "If 10 men brush against [the 370,000 female daily riders]," the official explained, "3.7 million accountable sins are committed every day."

The Russian government, seeking to improve the status of women across the country, appointed a man to head a special commission on the issue. "The commission is made up almost entirely of women," said a spokesperson for Deputy Prime Minister Oleg Sysuyev, the man named to the post, "so you need a man at the top to balance them out."

The Philippines government told women civil servants that if they want to avoid unwelcome sexual advances they shouldn't wear seductive clothes to work. Alma de Leon, the head of the civil service and one of the country's most senior women officials, reminded women workers of an official memorandum banning "tight-fitting, seductive, micro-mini and gauzy or transparent dresses" in government offices. Walking shorts, leggings, tights, and jeans are also prohibited.

The German town of Mari announced that it was replacing half the signs on the town's bicycle paths. Instead of all the signs illustrating the frame of a man's bicycle, half of them would be changed to show a woman's bicycle.

Afghanistan's fundamentalist Islamic religious police, formally known as the Department of Promoting Virtue and Preventing Vice, decreed that women cannot visit male patients in hospital wards that contain nonfamily members and must "refrain from hitting their shoes on the ground, which makes noises."

Young women drive almost as aggressively as men, according to an Australian study that found female drivers below age 30 are only slightly less likely than young men to tailgate, hurl abuse, shake their fists, blast their horns, and cut in front of other drivers. An aggression index, compiled from a survey by the Australian Associated Motor Insurers Ltd., shows young women scored 31.77 points on a road rage "Richter" scale, compared with men's score of 32.63.

The Savoy theater in Colombo, Sri Lanka, had to apply for government permission to restrict one showing a day of the movie *Kama Sutra*, based on the fourth-century Indian sex manual, to women only. After winning approval to discriminate against men, theater manager David Joseph said women packed the place.

A rabbinical court in Haifa, Israel, declared that married women must be home by midnight. The ruling was handed down in a divorce suit brought by a man who complained his wife hung out in singles bars and stayed out until morning. The newspaper *Yediot Ahronot* reported that when the woman defended her behavior by noting her husband was sleeping with other women, the court conceded such behavior was "insufferable" but insisted it is the wife who must be home by midnight.

Fairfax County, Virginia, Judge Robert Smith found Dr. Geraldine Richter not guilty of drunken driving, even though Richter admitted drinking four glasses of wine at a party before state police stopped her. She insisted she wasn't drunk when she used vulgar language and kicked a state trooper, claiming instead that premenstrual syndrome had made her irritable. The judge concurred.

French judge Huguette Le Foyer de Costil ruled that a female cast could perform Samuel Beckett's play *Waiting for Godot*, despite the protest of Jerome Lindon, the man designated by French law as guardian of the integrity of the late playwright's works. Lindon insisted that the play is about male characters and would be "deformed" by a female cast. The judge did order that Lindon's objections be read before each performance.

After Fayetteville, North Carolina, resident Lauren Cook Burgess, 35, sued to overturn a National Park Service ban on women portraying male soldiers in Civil War battle reenactments, the *Civil War News* ran a letter from a reader in Marietta, Georgia, calling women like Burgess who dress the part of Civil War soldiers "reenactor transvestites." Burgess dismissed charges that her portrayals thwart serious reenactors' efforts to ensure authenticity, noting, "I've had plenty of people mistake me for a man. I'll be in the women's room washing my hands and women will walk in and walk right back out."

When the European Community proposed a code governing sexual harassment in the workplace, a delegation of British women marched to EC headquarters in Brussels to voice their opposition. The women, all models who posed for British tabloids, feared the measure, which specifically bans nude pinups in the workplace, would cost them work.

In *The Women's Bible Commentary*, a compilation of the wisdom of "40 of the world's foremost female biblical experts," the story of Adam and Eve is seen in a different light. Eve is no longer "easy prey" for a dissembling snake. Her decision to take the apple is seen as a conscious act that brought her and her family knowledge and culture. Adam, on the other hand, is seen as rather limp in the feminist interpretation. "He takes the fruit from Eve without question," and when God accuses him of disobedience, he blames her.

The federal Occupational Safety and Health Administration cited the Pro-Line Cap Co. for having too few toilet facilities for its women employees and told it to rectify the situation. The Fort Worth, Texas, manufacturer of athletic caps fired 30 female workers. "We had two choices: to add toilets we could not afford or reduce the workforce," said Pro-Line attorney Franklin Sears, noting that the required facilities would have cost $25,000. "Adding toilets would take up needed production space, and we would have to lay off anyway even if we spent the money to comply with OSHA guidelines. Since the problem concerned only females, the only corrective action to take involved only females."

After frequent brawls among male members of Taiwan's National Assembly, women legislators joined the fray by screaming, trading slaps and kicks, and pulling one another's hair. The violence began when two members of the ruling Nationalist Party poked fun at opposition lawmaker Su Chih-yang after her underwear showed when she sat down. Nationalist lawmaker Kuo Su-chun berated Su, saying "As a woman you should also review your own behavior." Accusing Kuo of insinuating that she sat immodestly, Su walked to the podium and slapped her. Four other women joined the fracas, and a fifth collapsed from high blood pressure when she tried to stop it.

The Birds and the Bees

A 700-pound bull moose lumbered into a yard in Waterboro, Maine, and mounted a plastic foam deer used for archery practice. Police said the moose continued until the deer's head fell off, then wandered off in apparent confusion.

Officials of Florida Wildlife Park announced they were setting up mirrors around six flamingos because the birds are more sexually excitable if they're in a group.

Police in Rochester, New York, arrested a 33-year-old man twice in two months in incidents involving the man's attraction to cows on an area farm. In the first case, he admitted to authorities that he had indeed had sexual relations with one of the cows. In the second incident, after he was apprehended hiding in a cow barn, the man insisted that he was only there to count the cows.

The city manager and police psychologist of Cincinnati, Ohio, urged the city council to revise the test administered to prospective city police officers so that it would no longer ask whether the candidate had had sexual intercourse with animals. The two argued that the question was "not relevant."

Scientists at Great Britain's National Environment Research Council laboratories in Plymouth found that tributyltin (TBT) pollution affects the dog whelk, a shellfish common on British beaches between high-tide and low-tide marks, by causing females to grow penises and develop sperm ducts. So many have undergone this transformation that the whelks have been unable to reproduce and are dying out. The scientists reported that their experiment showed the more TBT the females are exposed to, the longer their new penises grow.

Ernest and Frances Haskins complained to a British court in London that they were kept awake at night because their neighbor's rabbits made too much noise mating. The court ruled that they did not have to hear the cavorting animals' constant "scratching, thumping, and banging," and the rabbits' owner, Joyce Hartley, agreed to build a garden shed to muffle their sound.

Patricia Wyatt called police in Key West, Florida, to report a stray potbellied pig was courting her husband's brand-new Harley-Davidson. While trying to have sex with the motorcycle's front wheel, the 50-pound pig scratched the paint and tore the bike's fabric cover, causing at least $100 damage. Animal control officers said the unclaimed stray would be neutered, but the bike's owner, Walter Wyatt, protested the punishment. "His crime is an

----

alleged sex act against a Harley," Wyatt said. "We don't even know if that's a felony."

Noting that the once-abundant white abalone was virtually wiped out by a commercial harvesting boom in the 1970s, as its prized meat fetched high prices, biologists in Ventura, California, reported that in the past two years they had managed to locate three of the mollusks. All were male. Gary Davis, a research biologist with the National Biological Service, explained that researchers trying to save the species cannot afford the extensive search required to find a female, if there even is one, without a grant, and they cannot get a grant until they have a breeding pair.

After Dutch researchers at the TNO-Nutrition and Food Research Institute in Delft exposed carp to a chemical found in sewage, the sex organs atrophied in the males and some developed an oviduct, which female fish use to lay eggs. Researcher Sylvia Gimeo said the chemical is responsible for feminizing animals, including fish and alligators, and other researchers suspect the same effect could be causing declining fertility among human males being reported in some European cities.

Babu, a 14-year-old Indian elephant at China's Zhengzhou city zoo, was engaging in amorous play with a female across a fence, according to the Xinhua news agency, when his trunk got caught and a large part was severed. Limb specialists summoned from across the country spent 17 hours reattaching the trunk.

Scientists at the South Pole found that female penguins make males pay to have sex with them. Payment is in the form of stones, which the females need for nest platforms. The researchers on Antarctica's Ross Island observed that paired females sneak away from their mates and approach the nests of unpaired males. After mating, the female grabs a stone to take back to her nest. Sometimes merely flirting with the single males will win females a stone.

Pollution may be feminizing wildlife, according to British scientists, who suggested that sewage treatment plants routinely release into rivers estrogen-like chemicals strong enough to cause the birth of hermaphroditic fish. Although there have been other studies of scattered animal populations with bizarre sexual defects living in polluted waters, the researchers from Brunel University and the British government called the frequency and severity of intersexuality in their study "both alarming and intriguing." The *Los Angeles Times* noted the problem is particularly perplexing because scientists don't know which chemicals are to blame, since sewage is a mix of wastes from homes and businesses, and the culprit could be anything from artificial hormones in birth-control pills excreted in women's urine to chemicals in pesticides and plastics.

To reduce the beaver population in the Wheat Ridge suburb of Denver, wildlife experts decided to use the long-acting contraceptive Norplant. As television cameras rolled to record the operation to implant the Norplant capsules in the first beaver, veterinarian David Robinson conducted a last-minute examination and ordered a halt to the procedure, declaring, "It's a male."

Keepers at Japan's Hamamatsu City Zoo were unsuccessful in getting a female gorilla pregnant because she and her mate didn't have sex often enough. They decided to try to arouse her by showing videotapes of wild gorillas mating. "The problem is that there aren't that many videos showing gorillas having sex," veterinarian Rikio Nakazawa explained. "If there were a porno video of gorillas, we'd really like to get our hands on it."

Hormone pills taken by a woman to rid herself of excess facial hair also made her pet rottweiler sexually obsessed with her. Writing in the British medical journal *The Lancet*, Leeds dermatologist John Cotterill said that the pills may have subtly changed the woman's body odor, so that the dog "would not leave her alone." The woman solved her problem by having the dog castrated.

Thieves in Wilmington, North Carolina, pushed a female dog through a window at a gas station, distracting the male guard dog inside while they made off with about a hundred old pennies, several rings, and a grinder. They left the bitch behind.

According to a case reported in the *Medical Aspects of Human Sexuality*, a 33-year-old woman was camping in Idaho with friends when she separated from the group to go into a portable commode to change her tampon. A young stag detected the scent, became sexually aroused, and charged the woman when she left the commode, knocking her down and hitting her shoulder repeatedly with his forefoot. After the deer sprayed her with semen, the woman's screams brought her friends, who had to shoot the deer to get him off his victim.

Florida's Department of Natural Resources recommended banning tourist attractions where customers pay to get into the water with captive bottle-nosed dolphins because adult males sometimes become sexually aroused and make sexual overtures to humans, including physical aggression and other aspects of the mating ritual. In one incident, a Miami legal secretary reported that soon after she entered the water, she noticed one of the dolphins rubbing against her in an unmistakably amorous way. She said the 700-pound animal spun her in the water and swam across her back, adding, "He liked me a lot."

In a study of ovine sexuality by University of California, Davis, graduate student Anne Perkins noted the difficulty of determining if lesbianism exists among sheep "because if you are a female sheep, what you do to solicit sex is stand still. Maybe there is a female sheep out there really wanting another female, but there's just no way for us to know it."

Condomania

Police in Waterford, Michigan, charged Keith Bradford, 34, with stealing a condom machine from the men's rest room at the Irish Tavern. "All we can figure is, he was anticipating a big weekend," a police spokesperson said.

New York City lawyer Timothy Mucciante was convicted of running a bogus investment scheme to trade condoms to Russia for chickens.

A chronic shortage of bottles in the region of Komi in Russia inconvenienced beer drinkers, who buy their brew on tap from tanks on the street, until they discovered that Russian-made condoms are the ideal receptacle. The condoms, whose thickness made them the butt of Russian jokes, can hold as much as three liters, far more than their flimsier Western counterparts.

Juan Cordova and Jose Guzman were arrested in Lima, Peru, for fraud. They reportedly gathered used condoms from a lover's lane, then washed and resold them as new.

The Contra Costa County, California, health department returned a shipment of condoms that had been earmarked for public health programs. Officials explained they were worried that the condoms' minty scent might promote fellatio.

Japanese researchers announced they had invented the singing condom. They put a microchip in the base of the condom that works the same as musical greeting cards, chiming the Beatles' "Love Me Do" at the vital moment.

A firm in Oakland, California, that was supposed to send customers Talking Condoms saying "Merry Christmas" instead sent ones that said "Thank you for your business." Marc Snyder, inventor of the Talking Condom and owner of the mail-order business, said a prostitutes' convention in Las Vegas was supposed to get a thousand of the thank-you condoms but got the Christmas condoms instead. He blamed the mix-up on non-English-speaking workers in his assembly plant, noting, "It's not a World War III kind of catastrophe."

Police in Indianola, Mississippi, charged Roger Townsend, 23, with stealing more than 3,000 condoms from the local health office. They found his pockets stuffed full of condoms when he was searched in connection with another case. Noting that the theft was unnecessary, since the health office distributes the condoms free, Indianola police chief Ken Winter said, "This case has to rank up there with the strangest we've ever handled. I just don't know what he was planning or what."

Officials of the Agency for International Development were curious when they spotted an unexplained 90 percent increase in the distribution of AID-supplied condoms to Egypt. Investigators discovered that many of the 50 million condoms being shipped there were being bought by wholesalers from large pharmacies that were supposed to be distributing them and resold to dealers in rural areas as toy balloons. "Because the condoms had been donated by the U.S. government," the agency's report explained, "they could be sold more cheaply than actual toy balloons, thereby undercutting competing products and generating profits for the Egyptian merchants."

When police in Sri Lanka arrested a man after finding a condom in his wallet, the medical director of the Family Planning Association, Sriyani Basnayake, protested to the police that "condoms are not a security threat." Police were skeptical, however, according to the state-owned newspaper *Daily News*, which quoted one officer as saying, "Why would anyone want to carry a condom in his wallet, unless of course he was up to some mischief?"

After the University of Pittsburgh asked its lawyers to determine whether it was entitled to royalties from condoms featuring on the package a panther resembling the university's mascot, Pitt officials sent a letter to Custom Condoms in Somerville, Massachusetts, demanding 6 percent of the gross sales.

The U.S. Patent and Trademark Office assigned a patent to Natalie A. Lerma-Solis for her idea for Condom Pocket Underwear for men and women. The undergarments have condom-size pockets, complete with zippers.

Merlyn Starley, a San Francisco chemist, patented "suspenders" that keep condoms from slipping off. It features two plastic clips and a special adhesive that attach to the user's legs.

Dutch politician Nel van Dijk asked the European Commission to reconsider its standard for the European condom because it does not take into account variations in penis size. The EC standard is 17 centimeters long and 5.6 centimeters across (6.8 inches by 2.24 inches).

Natural rubber latex, the stretchy material used in condoms and surgical gloves, is causing widespread allergic reactions. "Epidemics are not usually discussed in terms of contact allergy, but we are in the midst of one to natural rubber latex," Dr. Ronald R. Brancaccio of the New York University Medical Center said. He explained that the most common effect is a swelling in the genitals, but noted that life-threatening reactions can occur, citing the case of "a woman who went into anaphylactic shock after intercourse using a rubber condom."

The World Health Organization announced that stopping AIDS and other sexually transmitted diseases will require

20 billion condoms over the next decade. WHO researchers based their estimate on the assumption that men who need condoms for intercourse outside monogamous relationships would use 20 a year.

Condoms won't be used as evidence in prostitution cases in San Francisco, the district attorney's office announced. Before the policy change, when a condom was found in the possession of suspects charged with solicitation, prosecutors used it to help prove their cases. Supervisor Terence Hallinan, a chief supporter of the change, explained, "How can we be encouraging everyone to use condoms to stop the spread of HIV in this city on the one hand, when on the other hand we've been telling prostitutes that their use of condoms will be used against them in court?"

The French town of Condom, named for the confluence of its two rivers, stopped lamenting the ridicule its name evokes among English-speaking visitors, who pass through just to have their picture taken next to the town sign. Instead, the town decided to try to attract as many as 300,000 visitors a year by building a museum devoted to contraceptive devices used through history. Mayor Gerard Dubrac said the anticipated 1,800 sex-related items on display would make Condom the "condom capital of the world."

Twenty-five couples in Raleigh, North Carolina, tested a new loose-fitting plastic condom to see if it was more comfortable than the standard latex variety. The longer-lasting plastic condoms were said to resemble sand-wich bags.

Beginning in 1990, Danish Inter-rail passengers who bought tickets also received two free condoms and a leaflet telling them how to avoid getting AIDS as they travel around Europe.

The Northrup Corporation, manufacturer of the Air Force's B-2 Stealth bomber, formally urged the U.S. Patent Office to deny a trademark to the manufacturer of red-white-and-blue Stealth Condoms. The condom company wanted to sell them in a box shaped like the B-2. Northrup argued that the name "may falsely suggest a connection with" or bring "disrepute" to the military contractor.

Windsor, Ontario, reported that used condoms were clogging its new sewage treatment system. Officials said enough condoms eluded the system's filters each month to fill a 10-gallon bucket, causing backups at the Little River sewage plant, which serves a third of Windsor and four adjacent communities.

The newspaper *Argumenty i Fakty* reported that a Russian factory has introduced a line of painted souvenir condoms shaped like animals. One looks like a smiling tiger with the word "Hi!" painted on it, the paper said. There is also a series of condoms painted in the style of Russia's traditional blue-and-white Gzhel ceramics and shaped like teakettles, cups, and jars.

A judge in Toronto sentenced Charles Tumwesigye, 40, to 45 days in jail for sexual assault because he removed his condom while engaged in a consensual sex act. His partner had told him that she would only have sex with him if he wore the condom. In the middle of the act he decided to take it off and proceeded, despite her protests. Tumwesigye told police "it was too hard for me as a man to stop," and decided that since the woman did not push him away, it was okay to proceed. The judge noted that he would have made Tumwesigye's sentence longer if not for his "tragic" background—Tumwesigye was "pathologically afraid of the world" since witnessing a friend being decapitated by a tornado seven years earlier.

Spectator Sport

Four Californians were arrested for their conduct on board an American Airlines jet en route to San Diego from Zurich after a passenger and her 13-year-old daughter witnessed the married couple across the aisle from them having oral sex during the flight. After the woman alerted a flight attendant, two male passengers, whom police described as "voyeurs," began to throw food and drinks on the attendant to prevent her from stopping the sex.

The management of Toronto's SkyDome Hotel, which is adjacent to the stadium where the Toronto Blue Jays play baseball, had to post notices to occupants of the hotel's 70 rooms that overlook the field, reminding the people staying there that "the room in effect becomes part of the stadium, just as if it were a seat down below." That reminder was necessitated by a couple in one of the rooms who decided to stop paying attention about halfway through the game and make love instead—with the drapes open. Baseball fans noted that although the couple left the lights off, the stadium lights illuminated their lovemaking. At one point, witnesses said that much of the baseball audience stopped watching the game and watched the couple instead. According to the hotel manager, "I believe the people, for their own particular reason, wanted to perform in front of forty thousand people."

Olga Gennari, landlady of the 25-unit Tropical Garden apartments in Brasilia, instructed tenants to be quieter while making love. Noting that the apartments' lack of soundproofing means that bedroom noises "become public, above all if the heat of the event goes beyond the normal sense of emotion and love," her bulletin urged residents to "make a personal examination of your ethical, social, emotional, and sexual comportment."

Brazil's labor union officials, meeting to discuss ways to confront management's latest strike-breaking tactic, noted that officials at one mining company, Companhia Vale do Rio Doce, were enticing non-striking workers to stay on the job by showing them erotic films. The union leaders said they were considering countering the move by showing strikers the same films.

Cathy Baillargeon won a $12,000 settlement in her lawsuit, claiming that she was sitting on the toilet in the rest room of the Black Angus restaurant in Sacramento, California, when KROY radio disc jockey Dan Walker kicked open the stall door. He placed a microphone in front of her face to record her screams for broadcast.

Adult video stores reported the latest craze is homemade videotapes of ordinary people engaging in sex. "People like the amateur videos because they're more real than professional films," said John Ricardo, manager of Crazy Fantasy Video in New York's Greenwich Village. The companies marketing the tapes solicit new videos by attaching riders offering $10 to $30 a minute for raw footage that they turn into the finished product.

During a lawsuit brought by a woman against a 17-year-old Houston man who videotaped a sexual encounter between them without her knowledge, then showed the tape to some of his fraternity brothers, Judge David West ruled that the defense counsel Jaime Drabek could have a copy of the tape, but that only his colleagues and their experts could view the tape. Drabek lost the case, but after the verdict he showed the tape to as many as 16 other employees of his firm, Hirsch, Glover, Robinson & Sheiness. A subsequent investigation disclosed that Drabek also sent a copy of the tape to the defendant's insurance company, where at least four more people saw it. West fined Drabek's firm $2,000, but the indiscretion cost it an additional $600,000 when the girlfriend's attorney threatened to sue Hirsch, Glover for invading the woman's privacy anew.

A Singapore court sentenced Tan Ah-bah, 49, to three months in jail for assaulting a 37-year-old man. The incident occurred at a known lover's lane when the two men, who both admitted to being Peeping Toms, fought over the best spot to watch a couple making out in their car.

Police investigating a report of a light in an alley behind a home in Cheverly, Maryland, found a city-owned camera aimed at a second-floor bathroom. Police questioned a 58-year-old neighbor, who had access to the camera, and confiscated 191 videotapes, at least 10 of which showed people in his neighborhood using their bathroom. Police Sergeant E. W. Day said the person who did the videotaping got close enough to targeted windows that noises from the bathroom could be heard clearly on the tapes, noting "on some of the tapes, you can see all you'd want to and more." He said identification of some of the subjects was being conducted by "some county officials who know people in the neighborhood."

Jimmy Clarence Spiess, 53, of Slidell, Louisiana, was arrested for bugging the women's rest room of a bar and listening to conversations there while in his apartment above the tavern.

Sperm in the News

Cecil B. Jacobson, 55, a Fairfax County, Virginia, fertility doctor charged with impregnating at least seven of his patients himself, may have fathered as many as 75 children through what he claimed was an anonymous sperm donor program, according to Assistant U.S. Attorney Randy I. Bellows. Jacobson conceded that he was a sperm donor at his clinic on "a few occasions," but Bellows insisted that "according to employees, there never was another donor." The 53-count indictment by a federal grand jury stated that the doctor told patients, "God doesn't give you babies. I do." James R. Tate, one of Jacobson's attorneys, insisted that not only didn't his client do anything illegal but he actually may have done his patients a favor by not using other donors' sperm. "Their genetic heritage may, in fact, be superior to what they would otherwise have received," Tate explained. "The donor could have been a vagrant who carried the HIV virus and who sold his sperm to a 'sperm bank' used by Dr. Jacobson."

Authorities accused two staff members at New York's Mount Sinai Medical Center of running an unlicensed sperm bank in which they were the only donors. According to the state Department of Health investigation, medical resident Douglas Moss and center medical school lab director Jerald H. Tedeschi earned $9,000 by selling their semen to four doctors to use to artificially inseminate at least 17 women.

Julie Johnson, 34, a single navy lieutenant, gave birth to a 7-pound, 12-ounce boy on Mother's Day in Cary, North Carolina. She carried the baby as a surrogate for her sister, Janet Johnson, who was unable to get pregnant. After conventional fertility treatments and in-vitro fertilization failed, Janet sterilized a $2.95 turkey baster, collected semen from her husband, Mark Whittle, and gave it to her sister. Julie said she impregnated herself by standing on her head 30 minutes on two occasions, explaining, "I figured gravity couldn't hurt," Julie said.

Manhattan urologist Harry Fisch announced that, according to his research into sperm bank donations over the past 20 years, the quality of New York City sperm is better than Los Angeles sperm. Seeking explanations for L.A.'s lower sperm count, the *New York Observer*, which reported Fisch's findings with the comment "Yes, our boys can swim," quoted Joseph Feldschuh, director of one Manhattan sperm bank, who blamed the L.A. lifestyle: "Sexual frequency makes a difference. If you have an ejaculation every day, your sperm count drops."

Roger Short, a biologist at the Royal Women's Hospital in Melbourne, Australia, applied to the National Institutes of Health for funding to create mice that can produce human sperm. He told the journal *New Scientist* that the human cells would come from routine biopsies, such as those taken before surgery to reverse vasectomies.

Prison workers at the medium-security prison in Malone, New York, reported being splattered by semen that was mailed by prisoners to their spouses or girl-friends when the packets containing the fluid burst while going through the prison's mail machines. "It seems a case of, 'Darling, I love you and here's my semen to prove it,'" said Richard Edwards, Franklin County district attorney.

The Cryobank, one of the nation's largest sperm banks, with locations near UCLA, Stanford, and Harvard univer-sities, explained that it rejects 95 percent of the men who apply to be donors. It takes sperm only from men who are attending or graduated from a four-year college, prefer-ably an Ivy League school. "If our customers wanted high school dropouts, that's what we would get," said Cryobank spokesperson Ronda Wilkin, noting that a vial of sperm costs $135 to $165 regardless of the donor's alma mater. "No one has proven that Harvard, MIT, Princeton, or Yale sperm produces smarter children, but people like the idea."

Leland Traiman, a nurse in Oakland, California, announced that he was opening the Rainbow Flag Health Services, the nation's first sperm bank that accepts only homosexual and bisexual men as donors. "If a straight man wants to donate sperm, fine," Traiman said, "but I won't accept it."

A California appeals court awarded Deborah Hecht, 41, the 12 vials of sperm that her boyfriend, William Kane, left her in his will just before his suicide. After the man's former wife and two children claimed the vials should be evenly divided, a lower court awarded them three vials. The appeals court ruled that Hecht was entitled to all 12 vials, citing a dead man's right to procreate with the person of his choice as indicated by his written bequest.

A St. Louis appeals court denied a request by Steven Goodwin, 34, an inmate at the federal prison in Springfield, Missouri, that prison officials provide a container for his semen, which would be rushed to his 30-year-old wife so that she could have his baby. The three-judge panel said that granting Goodwin's request would be too burdensome and costly. What's more, Judge Frank J. Magill said, "If the [Bureau of Prisons] were forced to allow male prisoners to procreate, whatever the means, it would have to confer a corresponding benefit to its female prisoners."

Pamela Reno, 38, asked doctors at a hospital in Reno, Nevada, to remove sperm from her 19-year-old son, Jeremy, while he was on life support just before he died so she can become the grandmother of his child. Reno said she would seek an egg donor and carry the baby herself.

The *Straits Times* newspaper reported that dwindling stocks at Singapore's National Sperm Bank prompted a publicity campaign to attract donors, especially university students and soldiers. "We want a well-informed and receptive group of people who are also accessible," bank director Noel Long said.

Erwin Davis appealed his child-support order to the Arkansas Supreme Court, claiming his DNA matched the child's only because the mother broke into his home, stole a used condom from him, and inseminated herself. Unimpressed, the court upheld the order.

Britain's High Court denied Diane Blood, 30, access to her late husband's sperm, explaining that she would need his written permission—even though the sperm was taken from Stephen Blood while he lay hospitalized in a coma from which he never awoke.

A German company announced it had invented a new form of contraception for men. A small capsule implanted into both seminal ducts uses an electrical current to kill sperm before they leave a man's body. Neue Technologien said its Contraceptive Capsule requires no outside energy source. It contains a galvanized element that causes the seminal fluid to act as an electrolyte, killing the sperm when they swim over it.

Although its survey showed sperm counts worldwide have halved in the past 50 years, researchers at the Rigshospital in Copenhagen noted that Finnish men are producing twice as much sperm as everyone else. Finns also have a much lower incidence of testicular cancer and fewer cases of undescended testes. At the same time, the Finnish birth rate is one of the lowest in Europe, below the replacement level, and has shown little sign of increasing over the past 10 years.

After seven years in Italian courts, Luciano Anselmi of Cremona was told that he is legally entitled to disown his eight-year-old son, Mattia, because the boy was conceived with donated sperm. Anselmi initially agreed to the insemination, but within a year of the child's birth sought to have the marriage annulled and to disown the boy.

Canadians want to avoid the commercialized reproduction that occurs in the United States, according to a Canadian panel that recommended banning the sale of human sperm for profit. The report by the Royal Commission on New Reproductive Technologies noted that artificial insemination is a $164-million-a-year industry in the United States with almost no regulation. "We heard clearly from Canadians that they don't want market forces to determine how reproductive technologies are used in this country," said commission chairperson Patricia Baird, a medical geneticist from the University of British Columbia. "Canadians have looked south of the border and seen what happens when anything goes for a price."

A mechanical means of collecting sperm for medical use was touted as a moral alternative to masturbation, according to an article published by Catholic University of the Sacred Heart in Rome, which is under the direction of Italian bishops. Masturbation is the most common way to gather sperm for laboratory tests related to impotence and genetic diseases, but the Catholic church teaches that masturbation is immoral. The article described the use of a vibrating machine that attaches to a testicle, concluding from a survey of 17 men who used the machine that "several components that constitute the masturbation act would seem to be absent" such as "direct stimulation of the genital organ" and any "erotic feelings."

Retired University of Arizona law professor Jack J. Rappeport, who was sued by his cleaning lady, Maryann Ortiz, for fathering her child, did not deny paternity but insisted in court that he didn't recall ever having sex with the woman. Questioned by her attorney as to how he could be the child's father without having had sexual contact with Ortiz, Rappeport suggested artificial insemination ("She cleaned my office from time to time," he testified, "and there was refrigerated sperm in the refrigerator during that time"); when he was comatose ("There was a period of time when I was under heavy sedation for what has really never been truly diagnosed, but something that kept me from being able to walk"); or that she otherwise somehow had sex with him "without me being aware of it." Unconvinced, Judge Allen Minker ordered Rappeport to pay Ortiz about $500 a month in child support.

Sperm banks reported a spurt of deposits by U.S. troops heading to the Persian Gulf. "We had two to three hundred phone calls from military personnel," said Sharon

Coe, director of the Fertility Center of California. "One hundred have shown up."

Making sperm shortens worms' lives, according to a University of Arizona researcher. Graduate student Wayne A. Van Voorhies suggested that his study of nematodes might help explain why husbands live shorter lives than their wives. Calling it "a fascinating and a very clear observation," Dr. Philip Anderson of the University of Wisconsin, who studies the same worm, commented, "Those of us working with nematodes hold it as an article of faith that the genes and biochemical processes nematodes use are the same as those that humans and other mammals use. But, gosh, I hope it isn't true in this case. It would be awful to make the suggestion that one way to live longer is to castrate yourself at a young age."

Virtual Sex

New York City ambulance workers programmed an X-rated game into their computer system that could slow the computer or stop it for 30 minutes, according to a computer consultant for the Emergency Medical Services who was fired after he told his superiors about the threat to response time. John Petrofsky noted the game might also carry a virus that could shut down the computer. Officials acknowledged the sex-oriented game was on the system but disputed Petrofsky's claim it could delay response to emergency calls.

John Gordon of Bridgewater, New Jersey, filed for divorce, accusing his wife of using a computer to carry on a "virtual" affair. Attached to the divorce papers were dozens of E-mail exchanges, some sexually explicit, between Diane Gordon and a married man in North Carolina she met on America Online who called himself "The Weasel." The illicit relationship apparently wasn't consummated, although John Gordon claimed the two had made plans for their first real tryst.

Andrew Reding, 44, a city councilman in Sanibel, Florida, posted *Playgirl*-style photos of himself on the Internet, angering some residents in the conservative seaside community, who sent threatening and hateful E-mail. He explained he was simply looking for companionship and saw nothing wrong with the photos, which were digitally altered to include a strategically placed white square.

Warning elderly women not to accept phone calls from a man claiming to be their new physician, police in St. Paul, Minnesota, reported that the man called one woman and explained he needed to examine her over the telephone. He instructed her to disrobe and do several sexually oriented things, then he asked her to put on a light coat, go outside, and expose herself to a colleague in a car as he drove past. The woman told police afterward that she began to suspect something was wrong about the examination procedure when the man drove up in an old car.

After a series of threatening phone calls terrified some residents of a St. Louis suburb, authorities traced the calls to a pay phone used by inmates in the Essex County Jail in Newark, New Jersey. The investigators said they do not know why the calls were made or why the 27 Chesterfield, Missouri, residents who complained accepted the collect calls, which ordered them to perform sexual acts or told them family members had been kidnapped. Some victims hung up immediately, but others stayed on the line as long as 20 minutes.

Someone impersonating a police officer called a McDonald's in Milwaukee claiming that some money had been stolen from the restaurant. The caller convinced the female manager to strip-search a male employee to look for the money while holding the telephone to the man's genitals so the caller could "hear" the search.

After Kelly Lopez of Salem, Oregon, hired a private detective to find out who was regularly making obscene phone calls to her, the detective traced the calls to a telephone in a Marion County jail cellblock and learned that an inmate there had been calling Lopez collect. Authorities advised the woman that she could stop the obscene calls simply by refusing to accept the charges.

Dr. Jung Kao-fang of Taiwan's Chang Gung Memorial Hospital reported that the hospital had received 82 patients, 52 of them women, suffering from "lovemaking anxiety" caused by portable phones and beepers. "The phones would ring and beepers beep in the middle of their lovemaking," Jung said. "The husbands either hurried through or stopped to run out for business appointments."

German police arrested more than 60 people involved in a telephone sex ring. The suspects reportedly obtained large sums from telephone companies for providing a service that tricked callers into spending $260 million a year thinking they were talking live to telephone sex partners. Actually, up to 80 percent of the so-called conversations were prerecorded.

After a 12-year-old boy in Columbia ran up a $12,000 phone bill in one month by calling international sex lines, the phone company took steps to make sure there would be no repeat of the sky-high bills by suspending all international calls out of the working-class La Dorada district in Cali, the country's second-largest city. "I don't know what I'm going to do. I am selling our house, but even that isn't worth 12 million pesos ($12,000)," single mother Ana Maria Martinez told the NTC television news. She explained that her son, Juan Carlos, called sex-talk numbers in Israel, Lebanon, and Spain, staying on for as long as 30 minutes at a time, after seeing advertisements in pornographic magazines.

Undergarments

Japanese underwear maker Triumph International unveiled its tribute to classical composer Wolfgang Amadeus Mozart: an indigo bra (with matching panties) decorated with a musical staff and tiny lights that flash in time with an electronic music box that plays a Mozart composition. The lingerie is not suitable for daily wear, a company spokesperson said, because it isn't washable.

Hong Kong janitor Kung Man-wah, 33, was sentenced to 30 months in jail after being arrested when found wearing ladies' underwear in the women's changing room at the Kwai Chung police station. The *New Evening Post* reported the man admitted stealing the garments, as well as other bras and panties, from the same police station the day before.

A jury in Painesville, Ohio, found Van W. Patterson, 23, guilty of breaking into men's homes, fondling sleeping men, and cutting off their underwear. Dubbed the "BVD bandit," victims testified that they awoke to find their briefs and jeans slit across the groin, exposing their genitals. One of them said that he slept on the couch after an argument with his wife, who threatened to castrate him, and when he awoke and noticed his pants and underwear were cut, he assumed she had done it.

Police in Lincoln, Nebraska, said the arrest of Randy S. Boone, 37, ended a three-year wave of underwear thefts. In 24 instances, apartments were broken into and only underwear was taken. Underwear was also reported stolen from eight apartment laundry rooms.

Clerks at a Victoria's Secret store in Santa Barbara, California, said that when they turned to wait on other customers, a woman in the store made off with 500 pairs of panties, sizes medium and large, worth $5,000.

Tokyo police reported they were on the trail of the man (or men) responsible for accosting at least 13 women in the city and stealing their panties. In all cases, the women were just walking along public streets. None were injured in the incidents. In the most flamboyant of the attacks, a man in his twenties ripped the underwear from an 18-year-old woman and then jumped on a motorbike to make his escape.

A woman in Entiat, Washington, complained to police that while she and her children sat in a coin-operated laundry a man took off all his clothes to wash them. Sheriff's deputies took no action, explaining that the man was from Quebec, where such behavior is not unheard of.

A 46-year-old Los Angeles man accused of stealing women's underwear from clotheslines was apprehended by men in the neighborhood and turned over to the police. In the man's BMW police found 48 pieces of underwear and a woman's skirt. Later that day, the toilet in the city jail lockup backed up and overflowed, and five pairs of panties were found stuck in the toilet pipe. "He was probably wearing them," said Sergeant Paul Von Lutzow. "We don't do body searches on a misdemeanor."

The Salvation Army opened a special collection center in Dartington, England, for women to donate used brassieres to send to foreign countries. "In Russia, bras cost an absolute fortune," Carol Arthur, a Dartington recycling officer, pointed out. "And in India and Pakistan, the bra is a serious status symbol."

California artist Nicolino announced plans to embark on a coast-to-coast tour to collect 10,000 brassieres to span the Grand Canyon. He explained that "Bras Across Grand Canyon" would use large construction helicopters to drape a structural steel cable one mile across the canyon, then the bras will be attached directly to the cable or pulled across the canyon like underwear on a clothesline to create a bra bridge. "It's about the puritanical obsession with the breast," Nicolino said, adding, "I'm trying to keep it on the humorous side."

When smoke from forest fires in Malaysia increased air pollution to dangerous levels, a shortage of face masks resulted. Two government employees saved the day by recommending that people wear an improvised device made out of brassieres. News reports said the bras were much more comfortable and lasted much longer than regular face masks.

Charles Dupon, 52, was arrested for stealing 105 pairs of panties from one of his neighbors over the course of 16 years. Oxford County Police Supervisor Arthur Dean said that finally, "The woman realized, 'I buy a lot of underwear—where is it all going?' "

Germany's Defense Ministry announced that because so many recruits don't consider the standard army-issue starched-white underwear sexy enough, the army will offer a one-time payment of $25 so conscripts can buy their own briefs and undershirts. Everyone will continue to receive olive green underwear to wear in combat, however.

Australian scientists developed "air-conditioned" underpants specifically designed to be sperm friendly. The cotton garments resemble regular boxer shorts but have an inner mesh lining to provide a snug fit without damaging sperm the way conventional briefs do. "Some men I see with tight underwear don't like wearing boxer shorts because they don't like the freedom, the loose feel," said David de Kretser of Monash University's Institute of Reproduction and Development.

Battle of the Sexes

A Denver district court jury convicted Manuel Bustos Silva, 42, of murdering his common-law wife, Maria Rodriguez, despite his explanation that she hexed him by putting pubic hairs in his food, causing him to go crazy and strangle her.

Men are smarter than women, according to Richard Lynn, a professor at England's University of Ulster, who insisted, "The evidence is quite clear." He based his conclusion on the accepted fact that proportionally men have slightly larger brains than women, claiming that at least 11 recent studies have found a correlation between brain size and intelligence. Noting that twice as many men as women get top academic honors at Oxford and Cambridge universities, he said, "People have been trying to explain this in terms of sexist examiners, but it's because men are brighter."

On the other hand, University of British Columbia researcher Rosemary J. Redfield reported that males are the weak link in the evolution of the human species. Reporting in the journal *Nature*, the zoologist demonstrated that by mixing her chromosomes with a male's, a female perpetually tempts disaster because his sperm cells are 2 to 100 times likelier than her eggs to have mutations. Redfield explained that rather than help to

solve the controversy of why, given this propensity to
mutation, sexual reproduction evolved in the first place,
"my paper points out that the problem is worse than we
had thought."

A third viewpoint, advanced by University of Colorado
at Boulder physician and anthropologist Warren Hern, is
that humans of both sexes have become a "planetary
malignancy" that is growing out of control and devouring
its host, Earth. Hern, who said he reached his "planetary
malignancy" theory after 25 years of study, admitted, "It
doesn't make people feel real warm and fuzzy."

In the Dominican Republic, men and women voted sepa-
rately in the 1995 election, which was won by Leonal
Fernandez Reyna. Embassy officials in Washington
explained the separation was necessary because men are
rude to women, but the Associated Press reported it was
part of the plan to assure a fair election. Women lined up
at 6 a.m. to prove they were registered voters and started
casting their ballots at 8:30. Men gathered at 1 p.m. and
voted late in the afternoon. Once in line, voters couldn't
leave, which gave them no time to get to another polling
place to vote a second time. The result, officials reported,
was the cleanest election in Dominican history.

In Islamabad, Pakistan, a man was arrested for chopping
off his wife's nose during a domestic argument. "My
hands and legs were tied, and then my husband took a
kitchen knife and chopped off my nose," said Nursat
Parveen, 30, explaining that the husband became angry
when she criticized one of the couple's eight children for
not doing her chores. "Ignoring my cries for mercy, he

brought a kitchen knife and a pair of scissors and chopped off my nose and hair."

Women average 4 billion fewer brain cells than men, according to a 10-year study by Danish researchers. Dr. Bente Pakkenberg, a neurologist at Copenhagen's Kommune Hospital who headed the project, said she is baffled as to what the difference in nerve cells means. "Maybe we'll find it's much more important how they are connected than how many there are," she said, adding, "And if men have to have 4 million more brain cells to function as normally as women, it's all right with me."

Police in Peoria, Illinois, charged Christina Mack, 35, with greasing up the top of a stairway in her home in an attempt to make her one-legged boyfriend slip on the floor. Her plan backfired when she slipped on the floor instead and was knocked unconscious. After rescue workers revived her, police said she admitted hatching the scheme because she and boyfriend Chester Parkman, Sr., 50, had had an argument. Parkman at first agreed with her account, then changed his mind, telling police, "I honestly think she was trying to wax the floor."

The lawyer for Tushanee Priyadarshani told a court in Gampaha, Sri Lanka, that their client had been forced to live under a bed for most of the two years that she had been married because she declined to obey her husband. The newspaper *Island* reported that Ajith Pathmakumara ordered his wife to stay under a bed without food and water for several hours every day after she refused to worship the photographs of his idols, Sri Lankan cricket star Roshan Mahanama and Vijaya Kumaratunga, the assassinated husband of President Chandrika Kumaratunga.

A 22-year-old man in Durham, North Carolina, told police that while walking down a sidewalk he was abducted in broad daylight by two women wearing stocking masks. One woman knocked him down and held him while the other blindfolded him. They threw him into a van and drove around for about an hour before forcing him to undress, then took turns raping him every hour for the next 11 hours. They then released him near his home.

Twisted Trysts

A Prince William County, Virginia, couple finished watching an X-rated video at the 23-year-old woman's house, then decided to act out a fantasy involving a naked hitchhiker. After dropping her off, the 35-year-old man was supposed to circle the block and pick her up, according to police spokesperson Kim Chinn. "A car began to approach her and, thinking it was him, she jumped out in the road with her thumb out. But it wasn't him." The driver sped by and stopped at a fire station a half mile away. Firefighters sent an ambulance, which gave the naked woman a hospital gown and called police. After officers arrived, finally the man showed up, only to be charged with driving under the influence.

When a woman in Spain gave birth to twin girls, her husband suspected they resulted from an affair and demanded DNA testing. Tests showed that one of the nonidentical twins almost certainly was his child but that the other definitely wasn't. The woman later admitted she had sex with another man a few days after having sex with her husband. According to *The Washington Post*, only six other cases of twins with different fathers have been reported.

Lamont Hough, 24, was charged with impersonating his twin in order to have sex with his brother's girlfriend, but a jury in Mineola, New York, needed only five minutes to clear him, believing, despite the woman's claim to the contrary, that she was not fooled.

Shortly after Lu Shu-fang was crowned Taiwan's Miss Republic of China, she was stripped of her title for having been caught barefoot in a hotel room with a man.

Salt Lake City authorities accused Eric Lords, 20, of persuading a 16-year-old girl to marry him in a fake ceremony conducted over the telephone by a friend posing as a Mormon bishop. "She was tricked," prosecutor James Cope said, explaining the girl "did not want to have sex with someone who was not her husband."

After a court in Edmonton, Alberta, acquitted Marilyn Tan, 35, of charges stemming from injecting the AIDS virus into her former lover, photographer Con Boland, during sadomasochistic sex, Boland said that he held no grudge against Tan, telling reporters, "She has wonderful qualities."

Prosecutors in Prince William County, Virginia, dropped rape and sodomy charges against a 45-year-old man who told police that one of the victim's multiple personalities had consented to have sex with one of his multiple personalities. Citing insufficient evidence, prosecutor James

T. Willet said the man explained that since meeting the woman in group therapy, many of their different selves had fallen in love and even talked of marriage, including, in this instance, "Spirit," one of his 30 personalities, and "Laura," one of her many selves. "There was no forcing," the man insisted, "there was no hurting anybody. Spirit loved Laura."

The Virginia Department of Health Professions suspended the license of psychologist Robert L. Van de Castle, 69, who admitted engaging in improper sexual contact with two patients, including a woman with 11 personalities who later became his wife. The woman subsequently sued Van de Castle for harm and humiliation, charging he not only failed to cure her multiple-personality disorder, but also began charging admission to public displays of her different personalities.

The Egyptian government newspaper *Al-Massa* reported that an Alexandria woman who claimed she was too ill to fulfill her "marriage duty" drugged a woman friend to force her into having sex with the husband. Awakening after drinking drugged tea in the couple's house, the victim said, "I was stunned to find myself in the arms of my friend's husband in their bed." The paper noted police weren't certain what crime to charge the couple with.

Police in Fort Pierce, Florida, accused the mother and stepfather of a 15-year-old girl of trying to impregnate the teenager to make her the surrogate mother of their child. The mother, Gail Carrillo, 42, had undergone a tubal ligation but wanted a child with Francisco Carrillo, 30. They had sex at least twice while the mother watched, according to police, who explained that the girl agreed to have the baby so the couple would let her marry her boyfriend.

Former Riverside, California, high school football quarterback A. T. Page acknowledged having sex more than a hundred times with the 31-year-old wife of his coach, Randy Brown, 38, while Brown watched. Page explained that Brown claimed the interludes would make him a better football player, noting that while the couple were having sex the coach would start a videotape of a scrimmage or practice and tell him, "Now this is what you're doing wrong."

Clint Johnston, 69, facing charges in Mountain Home, Idaho, that he engaged in sexual activities with two 12-year-old girls, explained that he didn't know they were underage when they consented to have sex since he is legally blind and he couldn't see how old they were.

A Colorado couple filed separate lawsuits against a Boulder psychotherapist, whom they accused of breaking up their marriage. David Smith and Jane Harris said Jacqueline Jaeger was having an affair with Smith, one of her clients, while counseling Harris, another client, not to have sex with him. After Smith divorced Harris, he married Jaeger, although "under duress," Harris said, claiming that she also pressured him into giving up his federal civil service job to go into the roofing business with the therapist's brother. Court documents show that Jaeger had been fired from her previous counseling job for engaging in sexual relations and marrying another client, whom she later divorced.

Chris Ahamefule Iheduru, 47, was convicted in Dallas of having sex with his 14-year-old stepdaughter despite his testimony that he didn't know sex with a juvenile is illegal, since in his native Nigeria it isn't. Iheduru said he impregnated the girl after signing a contract with the girl to bear him a son on behalf of her mother, who is unable to have more children.

Two camp counselors in Copenhagen felt so sorry for two of their students who had been banned from attending summer camp that they arranged for a prostitute to entertain the boys, both 17 years old. The two teens shared the prostitute in the backseat of a school bus.

Authorities in Livingston, Montana, charged a 30-year-old mother of three who couldn't have any more children with arranging to have her boyfriend impregnate her 11-year-old daughter in hopes that the girl would bear a child she could raise.

Silvio Figueredo-Torres, 49, filed a $10-million suit against Bethesda, Maryland, psychologist Herbert J. Nickel for malpractice and intentionally inflicting emotional distress; to wit, having an affair with Figueredo-Torres's wife. Nickel denied having sex with Marsha Figueredo-Torres, 50, during therapy or before she separated from her husband, although just after the couple divorced he did marry her.

Silvio Figueredo-Torres's suit charged Nickel with demoralizing him by ridiculing him and telling him to stay away from his wife. During therapy, Nickel called him "a codfish" and said his wife deserved a "fillet." Nickel told the husband that he had bad breath and was to blame for the couple's problems.

To mark horse racing's $10-million Breeders' Cup races in New York, Pittsburgh radio station WDVE announced it would award $3,000 in cash and baby supplies to whichever one of four contestants, selected from 1,500 entries, became pregnant first.

British police announced they were seeking a man reportedly seen touching the genitals of a 12-foot bottle-nosed dolphin off the pier at the fishing village of Amble, Northumberland, in what they believe to be the first incident of a sexual assault on a dolphin. "There are several people involved," said marine zoologist Peter Bloom, who has seen injuries on the dolphin's penis that he concluded are the result of people encouraging the animal to use the organ unnaturally. "It's an increasing problem with tame dolphins in the wild. In Dingle Bay [Ireland] a few weeks ago I saw a stark-naked woman running into the sea shouting, 'Come on, Fungie, I love you.' Dolphins bring out the best and the worst in people."

Authorities in Laurel County, Kentucky, charged Jimmy Earl Humfleet, 33, with killing his uncle after he discov-

ered the uncle having sex with a pit bull. The shooting
was recorded on an audiotape of incoming 911 calls,
according to former deputy Derek House. In Humfleet's
first call, "He stated his uncle was having sexual intercourse with a dog, and he wanted somebody out there,
now," House testified at a preliminary hearing. When a
911 dispatcher called back a few minutes later for directions, Humfleet said nothing was wrong. Then he called
later to report his uncle was molesting a dog. The dispatcher heard arguing and a single gunshot. House testified that when Humfleet returned to the phone, he said, "I
shot him."

Israel Zinhanga, 28, told a Zimbabwe court that he had
sex with a cow because he was afraid of contracting AIDS
from a human partner.

Kim Lee Chong, 61, was sentenced to 15 years in jail for
trying to have sex with an elephant. After he was caught
naked from the waist down standing on a box behind the
animal, he claimed the elephant was the reincarnation of
his wife, who had died 28 years earlier. "I recognized her
immediately by the naughty glint in her eyes," Kim told
the court in Phuket, Thailand.

A man accused of having sex with a turkey at the poul-
try plant where he worked in Adams County,
Pennsylvania, admitted assaulting the 20-pound bird in an
employee shower but blamed his coworkers for encouraging him. After Timothy Bodkins explained that two
coworkers offered him $12 and three cans of chewing

tobacco to sodomize the turkey while one of them held it, District Justice John C. Zepp III fined him $750.

A 6-foot-tall, 150-pound female emu tried to mate with Ed Stuardi of Mobile, Alabama. The bird followed him around for several days, but when its intentions became known, Stuardi tried scaring it away by shooting his gun into the air. The bird continued hanging around, making deep noises in its throat that are a mating call, forcing Stuardi and his wife to cower in their house for two days. Finally, they called the authorities, who captured the emu and took it to a farm populated by her own species. "It was mating season, and she took a fond liking to him," said Diane Roberts, director of the Animal Rescue Foundation. "He had to ward her off with a boat paddle. She was absolutely intent that this was her mate."

The Big O

Insisting they can't have orgasms without sexual aids, six women filed suit to block a new Alabama law banning the sale of sex toys. Among the plaintiffs are Sherri Williams, who owns two stores that sell sex devices, and B. J. Bailey, who sells such items at get-togethers in women's homes, similar to Tupperware parties.

Mary Verdev, 73, sued a Milwaukee church for $90,000 after an electronic bingo scoreboard fell on her head. She claimed the accident caused her to become attracted to other women and to have spontaneous orgasms. A judge threw out the case when she refused to undergo a psychological exam.

A survey published in the Colombian magazine *Mujer* found that 40 percent of married women and nearly 70 percent of single women in the country fake orgasms during sex. "These figures show Colombian women have a serious problem," a psychoanalyst wrote in an accompanying article. "They show sexual dissatisfaction as well as significant inhibitions and mental barriers."

A pill that can produce the same sensation as orgasms may result from the discovery of a chemical that enables women who have suffered spinal cord injuries to attain orgasm. Rutgers University researchers Barry R. Komisaruk and Beverly Whipple, who in 1982 wrote the book *The G-Spot and Other Recent Discoveries About Human Sexuality*, isolated the vasoactive intestinal peptide, which Komisaruk believes triggers the orgasm sensation in the brain. "Contrary to what people may think," he noted, "we discovered that women in the study who were paralyzed and had no feeling below the breast area were, in fact, capable of having orgasm."

When dentists or anesthesiologists administer pain-killing drugs to patients who are taking the tranquilizers Valium or Versed, the patients may experience hallucinations that can make some of them believe their sexual organs are being fondled by the person treating them, according to Dr. John W. Dundee of Belfast. He also reported that some people who use the drug clomipramine experience orgasm when they yawn. One man said the orgasms tired him out so much that he had to lie down for 15 minutes after yawning, and a woman said she was able to become sexually aroused by deliberately yawning.

Police in Vinton, Louisiana, closed the Starz nightclub and arrested everyone involved in a fake-orgasm contest. The contest, inspired by actress Meg Ryan's scene in the movie *When Harry Met Sally*, in which she demonstrated how to fake an orgasm, was determined to be "lewd conduct" by the police in the audience.

Russian faith healer Boris Zolotov claimed to be able to induce orgasms in women using only his mind. His 10-day "healing seminars" attract hundreds, each paying 7,700 rubles to lie on a communal bed listening to American soul music while Zolotov shouts, "Who wants an orgasm?"

As the women shout back, "I do," Boris begins to concentrate and extends his arms. Then the women gather in a large circle and fling themselves around to the beat of the music at a feverish pace. According to reports, when the music stops, anywhere from 30 to 50 in a typical group are moaning on the ground in apparent sexual ecstasy. Some who have attended the seminars claimed that after working with Zolotov they can induce an orgasm in others by telepathy alone.

After Canadian police arrested a 23-year-old woman in British Columbia who led them on a high-speed chase, she insisted she suffered from a "sexual speed fetish" and had been masturbating throughout the 120-miles-per-hour pursuit. "I can only come when I smell the aroma of hot tires," she explained. After being ordered to seek psychiatric counseling, she said she would buy rubber panties, hoping they have the same erotic smell.

British doctors Robert Will and Paul Reading of Edinburgh's Western General Hospital reported they cured a 44-year-old woman of her orgasms. The unidentified woman "would suddenly become aware of an internal, ascending feeling indistinguishable from an orgasm," the doctors wrote in the medical journal *The Lancet*, noting it cropped up without warning, sometimes while driving. She complained only after one episode left her unconscious.

Therapists at London's Institute of Psychiatry reported the results of "orgasmic reconditioning" they performed on a 20-year-old patient named George. Originally sexually preoccupied with urination by dogs, children, and women, George came to the institute able to become sexually aroused only while sitting in the family car, an Austin Metro, or when squatting behind it with the engine running. Writing in the journal *Sexual and Marital Therapy*, the therapists claimed partial success by getting George to switch his masturbatory stimuli from the car to photographs of naked women.

Picture This

When Wendy Ellington announced she was suing a Tampa, Florida, drugstore, whose photo developers copied a set of nude photos of her taken by her boyfriend, then circulated them at parties, about 150 frantic women called Ellington's lawyer, Matthew Powell. He had come into possession of several albums of nude photos, and the callers wanted to know if their nude photos were part of the collection. Ellington found out about the pictures when her boyfriend went to a party and spotted their pictures in the host's photo album.

When the Iranian weekly magazine *Fakhur* (meaning "Thinker") published photographs of Gennifer Flowers, Paula Jones, and Monica Lewinsky as part of a story about President Clinton's sex scandal, a Tehran court fined editor Reza Ghanilu $300 for obscenity because the women were pictured without veils, as required by Islamic law.

The French Health Ministry announced it spent $63,000 to help finance five hard-core pornographic movies for pay-TV. "They are totally explicit," ministry spokesperson Annette Omblari said, explaining that in return for the government funding, the films must promote safe sex. "I had to show that if a man has sex with two women together," director Lucile Hadzihalovic said, "he must use a different condom with each one."

Thai censors objected to a Bangkok film festival showing a New Zealand comedy *Topless Women Talk About Their Lives.* After festival organizers protested, the board of censorship agreed the film could be screened but only if objectionable scenes were blocked by having the projectionists put their hands in front of the projector.

When an East Detroit woman halted an affair with Eric Sanderson in order to reconcile with her husband, the man reportedly attached about 50 videocassettes to windshields of neighbors' and the woman's relatives' cars. The tapes contained sexual scenes featuring the two of them. He was also accused of distributing crude cartoons that he drew of him and the woman in sexual situations.

A Salt Lake City restaurant found three Polaroids of a man exposing his genitals taped to its drive-through window in January. Police speculated that unusually cold weather had forced the flasher to use this substitute method.

Official outrage in Britain boosted sales of a videotape that consists of excerpts from security cameras. *Caught in the Act* shows couples having sex in unlikely locations such as department store changing rooms; robberies; and drug dealers fighting each other. "We sold 60,000 in the first morning" after Parliament objected to the first tape, James Hunt, one of the video's researchers, said. "We've ordered another 125,000 copies." When a sequel, *Really Caught in the Act*, prompted more complaints from Parliament, Hunt exclaimed, "We're hoping we can keep this going."

Morris County, Kansas, Sheriff Corky Woodward, 32, rented a camera and videocassette player from his local video store, took it home, and made a 90-minute sex tape featuring himself and his wife. He returned the equipment to the store but forgot the tape was still in the VCR. The next customer to rent it saw the tape and made a copy. Soon as many as 200 copies were circulating all over the sheriff's hometown of Council Grove, and the owner of the video store was deluged with requests from other video stores for copies of the tape. Press interest spread all the way to New York City, and the sheriff went into seclusion while some townspeople considered a recall petition.

After repeated complaints to the police about a man who peered in her kitchen window at her and masturbated "almost daily" for five years, Betty Napier of Stuart, Florida, took matters into her own hands. She set up a hidden video camera, which caught the culprit in the act.

Police conceded that they are powerless to stop the dramatic increase of men secretly videotaping up women's skirts and down their blouses, even though some of the pictures are posted on the Internet, because as long as the taping occurs in public, it's legal. Spokespersons for an Irvine, California, Web site that publishes some of the photos said they are responding to society's fascination with surveillance and seeing forbidden pictures. "Men used to bring down a head of an animal as a trophy. Now it's panties," Robert Roy, 25, who works for the company that runs the site, said. "This is a high-tech, urban form of hunting."

Sony Corporation announced that it was halting shipments of some versions of its Handycam video cameras after published reports that the cameras could be used to see through clothing. The cameras in question were equipped with infrared technology to take night shots, but when the special feature was used in daylight or a lighted room with a special filter, it reportedly revealed lightly dressed people's underwear and made people in swimsuits look almost naked.

Some residents of a Bexley, Ohio, neighborhood announced their objection to tearing down an adult video store and replacing it with a McDonald's. Noting that the video store didn't create much traffic and that patrons were usually well dressed, opponents of the development proposal warned that McDonald's would bring traffic, noise, odors, and trash. Activist Steve Elbert explained, "We think fast food is equivalent to pornography, nutritionally speaking."

The Smithsonian Institution shredded more than a hundred pounds of photographs of thousands of Yale

University students who posed nude for a research project to study the relationship between body shape and intelligence. From the 1940s through the 1960s, Yale and other Ivy League schools allowed researcher W. H. Sheldon to take frontal and profile photos of their students. Although Sheldon's work has been dismissed by most scientists as quackery, his photographs wound up at the Smithsonian, which never displayed them publicly but did make them accessible to students and researchers. When Yale officials learned that the photographs still existed, they asked that access be cut off and photographs of its students destroyed to protect the privacy of its graduates, many of whom have gone on to become recognized leaders in culture and politics.

When Portugal's Channel 4 was launched as a station with "humanistic and Christian values," priests and church organizations urged people to buy shares and make contributions. Four years later, many of the station's 12,000 Roman Catholic investors had become upset because it tried to boost revenue and lure viewers with broadcasts featuring sex and violence. One promotional campaign announced "We've changed," then showed topless women and violence.

Convicted child molester Robert H. Ellison, 65, petitioned a Chicago judge for the prompt return of his child sex videos. He explained he feared he would molest more children if he could not relieve his urges through pornography.

Long Islander Marion Frankson, 41, was accused of having sex with her daughter's 16-year-old boyfriend in the backseat of a car while her husband, William, 42, videotaped them from the front seat. The Franksons propositioned the boy, apparently without the daughter's knowledge, when she brought him home to meet her parents, police said, adding that the boy wore a mask during the taping so he would not be recognized.

Police in Buffalo, Missouri, who found videotapes at a video-rental store of 83 local women posing nude at a tanning salon said the women were secretly videotaped while tanning, using a two-way mirror and a camera in the upper corner of a wall. Sheriff's authorities confiscated the tapes, but Sheriff Jerry Cox made no arrests, even though his daughter and daughter-in-law were among those taped. Dallas County Prosecutor Wayne Rieschel, whose wife and daughter appear on the tapes as well, told Cox he could find no state or federal law dealing with secret videotaping.

The German television talk show *Schreinemakers Live* turned the tables on Bryce Taylor, the man who rigged a camera in the ceiling of his London gym and took pictures of Princess Diana weightlifting wearing leotards and bike shorts. The program secretly videotaped him watching a sex movie in a hotel room.

A Prince George's County, Maryland, grand jury indicted a 32-year-old woman for rape, incest, and pornography for having sexual intercourse with her 9-year-old son. The chief evidence against her was a videotape she made of her fondling and having intercourse with her son.

After Grand Haven, Michigan, video store owner David Wingate Sr. was acquitted of obscenity charges last winter, he demanded that police not only return the eight X-rated tapes undercover agents rented to obtain evidence against him, but also pay nearly $8,000 in overdue rental fees. "Business is business," Wingate said.

The British Broadcasting Corporation paid a married couple $18,000 to make love three times a day for three weeks for a television documentary. To film the act of lovemaking from a different perspective, Wendy Duffield, 31, had a stainless steel camera the size of a ballpoint pen fitted inside her, and her 38-year-old husband Tony had a tiny camera strapped to his penis.

A 14-year-old boy who was alone at home in Ridgefield Park, New Jersey, ordered an adult videotape from a video delivery service. A skimpily dressed woman showed up and demanded $250. The boy told police that when he could only come up with $27, the woman threatened to have him killed and took the family stereo.

Bowing to public pressure, a Swedish court stopped selling child sex videotapes, which it had been making available under Sweden's freedom of information rules. District court officials had been holding free film shows and had received 33 orders for some of the 78 videotapes that had been confiscated as obscene. When demand for the tapes prompted court officials to ask police officers to help make copies, national police chief Bjorn Eriksson refused, saying it was the job of police "to catch pedophiles, not sell their wares."

A former alderman in River Falls, Wisconsin, and his wife pleaded guilty to secretly videotaping young women taking showers at their home. The women were foreign exchange students staying with the couple. Police found a total of 16 videotapes containing footage of 108 shower scenes featuring 62 different women.

A 54-year-old Italian schoolteacher was arrested for trying to sell as many as 700 homemade videotapes of couples having extramarital sex. The teacher was popular in his village of Striano for offering his home for trysts, but he would secretly tape the sessions and offer them for sale in Naples, where he presumed the subjects wouldn't be recognized.

Odds and Ends

The New York Times reported that Egyptian conserva-
tives accused Israel of waging a sex war against their
country, citing pornographic videotapes, explicit pop-
music cassettes, and even Arabic-language advertising for
a phone-sex line that have made their way from Tel Aviv
to Cairo. Even *Rosa el Youssef*, the Egyptian magazine
that was banned in parts of the Arab world for publishing
pictures of bikini-clad women, condemned the phone-sex
ads as an Israeli ploy to corrupt Egyptian young people.

The furor reached new heights, according to the
Washington Post, when police in Mansoura launched an
investigation into the sale of chewing gum reportedly
laced with a powerful aphrodisiac. Some Egyptian newspapers identified the distributor of the gum as Israel.
Fathi Mansour, who represents the city in parliament,
claimed he knew of 15 cases in which women and girls
had sexually assaulted men after chewing the gum,
explaining he learned about the aphrodisiac after speaking with neighbors who gave it to their wives "as an
experiment." Calling the gum "a plan to finish off Egypt's
youth," Mansour added, "Probably men want lots of this."

When county supervisors threatened its budget, Nassau
Community College in Hempstead, New York, agreed to
modify a controversial course on sexuality. College offi-

cials axed visits to gay bars, interviews with prostitutes, 80 slides of male and female genitalia, and such homework assignments as taking a bubble bath and masturbating. They said students still would see an explicit film on sexual intercourse.

Following reports that a woman who never had sex was artificially inseminated in England, some Christian clergy there denounced virgin births as immoral.

Sexually conservative students at Oxford University's Exeter College appointed third-year classics student Roger Evers to patrol the campus in an effort to stamp out public kissing, cuddling, and excessive displays of affection. Undergraduates also voted to ban heavy petting in the dining room and to split the junior common room into two areas, one for heavy petting and one for light petting, and supported a motion banning sexual intercourse in the college library between three and eight in the morning. Asked if sex in the college library was a common relief from the boredom of studying, student Alex Potts replied: "It hasn't happened to me yet, but you live and hope."

An anti-U.S. demonstration outside the U.S. Embassy in London was peaceful until Elizabeth Begaud, 40, of Lafayette, Louisiana, emerged from the embassy at lunchtime and gestured at the 200 Somali protesters. Then she hiked her skirt and flashed her thighs, provoking a melee, during which several women in the crowd attacked her, pulling her to the ground, and tugging at her hair. After restoring order, police charged Begaud with disorderly conduct and using threatening, abusive, or insulting words or behavior.

Eggs were stolen from at least nine women who were anesthetized for what they thought were routine diagnostic surgical procedures at the University of California at Irvine's Center for Reproductive Health, according to the *Orange County Register*. The paper reported the ova were implanted in other women and resulted in three births.

Nunzio Saita, 70, a priest in Caltanissetta, Sicily, received a suspended prison sentence and had his church bell confiscated after a couple in the town complained that his excessive bell ringing was ruining their sex life.

Russian workers at the Akhtuba factory in Volgograd received their salaries in rubber dildos, according to *The Economist*. The factory had switched from making marine navigation equipment to making the rubber goods, which it hoped to sell to local sex shops. Instead, it was stuck with the sex toys, the magazine reported, because "the market had moved on to electronic vibrators, and insert dildos were unsaleable."

Baseball's minor-league Charleston (South Carolina) RiverDogs offered fans the chance to win a free vasectomy as a Father's Day promotion, only to withdraw the offer the next day after fans protested. Among those who

complained was the Roman Catholic Diocese of
Charleston, led by season ticket holder Bishop David
Thompson. "We found that clearly people didn't like the
idea," General Manager Mark Schuster said, noting the
team never meant to offend anyone. "We are sensitive to
our fans' wants."

A bearded woman and a female friend were shot to
death in a karaoke bar in Portland, Oregon. Witnesses
said Barbara J. Gilpin, 44, and Jacqueline Julita Anderson,
29, argued with a man, who left but returned several
hours later with a shotgun and opened fire. Manager
Heather Foong said it appeared that the man had a relationship with Gilpin and was jealous of her bearded com-
panion. "I think he thought she was a man," Foong said.
"The police officers thought it was a man at first. It was
some kind of problem she had all her life, I think."

Police in Denver detained a 50-year-old postal clerk after
he came to work wearing a dress, gorilla mask, and a
"strap-on sexual device." Told by his superiors to leave
work, the man returned with several guns and began making threats.

Police in Belle Glade, Florida, recorded the following
criminal complaint: "Victim stated she had gone up to suspect's room to drink some wine. After, in the suspect's
room, the suspect left to get some more wine and locked
her in the room. After suspect returned they mutually
agreed to have sexual intercourse. Victim stated she was
on her hands and knees on the bed when the suspect

attempted entry, missing his main mark and struck the victim in the anus, driving her out of a second-story window. The victim was unable to move from the waist down after the fall; however she was very talkative. She kept shouting, 'That motherfucker tried to fuck me in my asshole.' Victim was found with her clothes down around her upper thighs. Victim taken to Glades General Hospital by ambulance. Writer spoke with suspect who confirmed incident. Both victim and suspect very intoxicated."

Army Colonel Edward L. Modesto, 42, was charged with conduct unbecoming an officer after being accused of committing homosexual acts and wearing a wig and women's clothing while exposing himself to customers at Laundromats. Court documents showed that Modesto, a dental surgeon at Fort Carson, Colorado, performed at a gay bar as a drag queen named Carmen while dressed in wigs and sequined gowns and lip-synching Bette Midler songs.

Researchers reported they had discovered the first physical difference between homosexual and heterosexual women: lesbians' hearing systems work more like those of men. "Their auditory centers have been masculinized and the presumption is that so have the sites in the brain that direct sexual preference," said Dennis McFadden, one of the researchers at the University of Texas at Austin.

Authorities at London's Central Criminal Court said that three men who had been arrested for raping Sandra

----

Harris, 25, were falsely accused. Harris admitted she is a
lesbian who had sexual intercourse with a man because
she wanted to have a baby, then fabricated the rape story
because she could not face her female lover.

Men with more ridges in fingerprints on their left hand
than on their right hand are likelier to be homosexual,
according to two researchers at the University of Western
Ontario. Their findings were based on a comparison of
fingerprint patterns in 66 homosexual men and 182 heterosexual men. Since fingerprints are completely developed in human fetuses by about the sixteenth week after
conception and are largely genetically determined,
researcher Doreen Kimura said the study "certainly suggests sexual orientation is somehow determined by pre-
natal events."

After the Right Reverend David Hope, the bishop of
London, announced that he was sexually "ambiguous," he
was promoted to the Church of England's second-highest
post, archbishop of York.

A 31-year-old New Yorker targeted the citizens of
Clarksburg, West Virginia, as recipients of more than 300
letters detailing his daily homosexual sex life in New York
City and his unbridled contempt for their existence. The
writer, using the pen name J. T. Colfax, labeled his daily
letters "art" and mailed them at random to Clarksburg residents picked from a telephone book. Explaining that his
art project is an attempt to introduce homosexuality into
small town America, Colfax said he picked Clarksburg

because it had no gay bars and so angered local folks wouldn't be able to vent their hostility at anyone specific.

Police in Key West, Florida, had to be called to break up an argument between a 28-year-old woman and a 29-year-old woman, whom the first woman accused of trying to steal her "strap-on deluxe model" vibrator.

Nina Hartley, a porn star who calls herself a Berkeley feminist bisexual sex industry worker, reacted to the Starr Report by calling the $40-million investigation "the biggest publicly funded porn production I've ever seen." The *San Francisco Chronicle* reported that when Hartley learned Monica Lewinsky gave the president oral sex while he was talking on the phone with congressional leaders, she commented, "That's nervy. If he can multitask like that, more power to him."

While Russian ultranationalist Vladimir Zhirinovsky was being interviewed for *Playboy* magazine, he repeatedly propositioned the female reporter and her 20-year-old female interpreter while the interviewer's tape recorder was running. "We'll understand one another better if you undress right now," he said. "You will lie on these little beds, and these boys [his bodyguards] will caress you. And I will be listening to you and continue talking myself."

He went on to suggest that sex was "best when it's with a group. There are four of you here. You have to show me love for four. I love to watch more. . . . I can join you later during the process. For me it's a way to get excited." He proceeded to urge the reporter to go to bed with him "for the sake of your profession, to get to know better the person you are writing about . . . during the coitus I would talk more."

A letter printed in the Ann Landers syndicated column in March 1982 expressed a mother's concern for the games being played in her house by her 14-year-old daughter and the daughter's 14-year-old boyfriend. "They have one unusual activity that I find hard to understand," the mom wrote. "He likes to tie her up, and obviously she likes to be tied. He treats her very gently when he ties her, although she often gets tied into some very stringent positions. They often spend hours inventing new positions and new ways to tie her. Some evenings they watch television for hours while she is tied rigidly to a chair. They seem to keep this hobby of theirs to themselves, but are open about it at his house and ours. His mother and I have discussed it. She feels it is just their way of having fun. I find it quite interesting to watch them and am amazed at how many ways a person can get tied up. On two occasions I let them tie me up—once to a chair and once to a post. I found it to be a fascinating sensation."

In her response Ann Landers said, "The fact that you became part of the act is another strange one. And the boy's mother knows and approves. More oddities. I suggest you talk to a therapist about this."

Sources

Agence France-Press
Anchorage Times
Arizona Daily Star
Associated Press
Bangkok Post
Bloomington Herald
  Times (Indiana)
Boston Globe
Chicago Tribune
China Post
Clarion-Ledger
  (Jackson,
  Mississippi)
Columbus Dispatch
  (Ohio)
Crawdaddy
Daily Yomiuri (Japan)
Daily Universe
  (Brigham Young
  University)
Dallas Morning News
Denver Post
Duluth News-Tribune
The European

Evening Telegram
  (Superior, Wisconsin)
Farmington Valley
  Herald
Fairfax Journal
  (Virginia)
Fortean Times
Gannett News Service
Globe & Mail (Toronto,
  Canada)
Hartford Courant
  (Connecticut)
Houston Chronicle
The Independent (U.K.)
Kentucky Gazette
Knight-Ridder News
  Service
The Knoxville News-
  Sentinel (Tennessee)
Los Angeles Daily
  News
Los Angeles Times
Medical Aspects of
  Human Sexuality

Miami Herald
Minneapolis Star
  Tribune
Montgomery Journal
  (Maryland)
National Lampoon
New York Daily News
New York Newsday
New York Post
New York Times
Newsweek
Orange County
  Register (California)
Orlando Sentinel
  (Florida)
Philadelphia Daily
  News
Philadelphia Inquirer
Playboy
Post-Standard
  (Syracuse, New
  York)
Raleigh News &
  Observer (North
  Carolina)
Reuters
Rocky Mountain News
Salt Lake Tribune
San Francisco
  Chronicle
San Jose Mercury
  News (California)

Scripps Howard News
  Service
Seattle Times
St. Louis Post-Dispatch
St. Paul Pioneer Press-
  Dispatch
St. Petersburg Times
  (Florida)
Star-Ledger (Newark,
  New Jersey)
Sun (Baltimore,
  Maryland)
Syracuse Herald-
  Journal (New York)
Texas Monthly
Time
Times-Picayune (New
  Orleans, Louisiana)
Toronto Star
Tribune Chronicle
  (Ohio)
Tulsa World
United Press
  International
U.S. News & World
  Report
USA Today
Wall Street Journal
Washington Post
Washington Times
World Press Review